The Writings

2020 -2022

JayneeAM

The Writings 2020 -2022
JayneeAM

First published in Australia by Jayne Miller 2022
https://jaynee.com.au/blog/

A catalogue record for this
book is available from the
National Library of Australia

ISBN: 978-0-6482369-2-4 (pbk)
ISBN: 978-0-6482369-3-1 (ebk)

Cover art by Gail Fay © 2022

Typesetting and design by Publicious Book Publishing
Published in collaboration with Publicious Book Publishing
www.publicious.com.au

Disclaimer:
The writings were created during morning meditations. To preserve the authenticity of what came to me I presented them as close to their original format as possible. The method of writing was often an unconventional stream of consciousness with multiple interpretations. I chose to use poetic license so that the uninterrupted flow of the writings would better engage the reader to ponder their own interpretations from what was shown to me.

Dedication

These writings are dedicated to Heather Scott who passed away at 4 am on 28th February 2022 when the whole side of the mountain in Upper Wilson's Creek Rd Mullumbimby collapsed. This happened during the most tragic that Northern Rivers New South Wales Australia.has ever known. Heather will be forever in our hearts and minds forever as she marks a point in time on this planet, never to be forgotten,never to be repeated and one day atoned for when the truth is finally revealed. Heather was married to Michael Edward Scott known as the beloved Archangel Michael. She was his widow for twenty years after his passing.

Many of us drew comfort and strength from Michael's writings for humanity over the thirty years we knew him. I was so grateful to Heather for making sure his writings were available to us all. We love and treasure both Heather and Michael and are forever blessed to have known them. I have chosen one of Michael's "messages for humanity" in its original format to add to these writings.

The Sinister Supression Of Freedom

Beloved humanity, how misguided we have been and are being in the search for freedom. How hypocritical and selfish we have become in the search for a better existence.

What blinding ignorance we create when our attention is diverted by the sinister and insidious so called "ANTI CAMPAIGNS" that tell us how to live our lives and which seek to control and manipulate the mass of human presence, all for greed of power.

Humanity cries out for freedom in one voice, yet seeks to control others in many voices and many ways. Parents seek freedom for their children, yet place their beloved offspring in the supposed care and controlling manipulative hands of governing bodies in the hope of a better education in life, so as the child may grow into a free spirit (Oh! What a gown of deceit hypocracy wears).

When it is in truth the best education of freedom is life itself experienced through the freedom of CHOICE within each individual expression of humanity, and not through the manipulative control by a cluster of power seeking governing bodies.

Not all are blameful and not all are blameless as they whom have allowed this to occur carry as much responsibility as they whom perpetrate and have created this situation, and it has been occurring for centuries.

How sad and truly selfish, we as a species place the lives of the children and future generations in the controlling grasp of governing bodies, that one day may use the children as cannon fodder and weapons against other humans only to gain more control and selfish power.

"Oh! How tainted and dark the soul whom uses and abuses other souls to wreak harm unto another."

Now we as a species are moving into the 21st Century as recorded time is perceived. We as a species claim to aspire for a better existence yet we cling tenaciously to old and narrow ignorances, then give them titled excuses through religious, political and fundamental ramblings.

As we move into the 21st Century one of the most underlying and insidious manipulative ignorances is the so called Anti Campaigns, as they are so subliminal that they distract the vast mass of Human Awareness to focus on supposed negative outcomes through individual free choice, so as to make the individual feel unworthy, guilty and fearful for being. While they of the "Born Again" moralistic crusader mentality get swept away once again by the Principal of Deception (manipulative control).

I am one of many whom are very much opposed to the destructive negative actions and thoughts of the human species yet I am a realist in the sense that I am aware that it is not the individual choice of personal experience that poses a threat to Humanity and Creation itself, but is in truth the negative focus placed upon the negativity in being. For example: It is so astounding the amount of people whom have acquired tobacco related diseases ever since they (the manipulators) have told Humanity of the diseases it MAY create."Tell the masses it's evil and they will manifest its evilness." "Tell the masses it creates disease and Dis-ease they shall create."

It is equally astounding that we do not hear of the millions of people whom do smoke tobacco and live long happy and healthy lives. For they do exist.

I am very much opposed to the wanton taking of human life, therefore I am opposed to wanton abortion, yet the circumstances must be weighed and for any individual, especially male individuals to deny a female the freedom of choice on this matter is more heinous and sinister than the individual choice will ever be.

Then there is the anti-homosexual movement. How dare the ignorant claim that only their chosen sexuality be the only natural one, as it is as natural for a homosexual to be homosexual as it is for a heterosexual to be heterosexual or a bisexual to be bisexual.

This anti-homosexuality stems from bygone antiquated religious and spiritual ignorant philosophies obviously brought into being by a Homo Phobic.

These are but examples of the Anti Campaigns which are still circulating.

When shall the masses realize that these Anti Campaigns are truly persuasive, attention, fear mongering to sway our rationale away from the true dark and malign negativities of the Human species such as nuclear weaponry, germ warfare, legalized murder, suppression and oppression. The list is endless and the basis is greed and the want of manipulative control. If it is that any feel the need to be Anti, then be Anti anything that is Anti FREEDOM OF CHOICE and allow us all to grow and take the responsibility for our choices that we as individuals take, cease blaming others for the choices that we make ourselves through our own individuality of being.

"What is poison to one, may be honey to another."

Take heed they whom title themselves Christians, whom have joined the Anti Campaigns for your choice is truly ANTI-CHRISTED.

Amen,

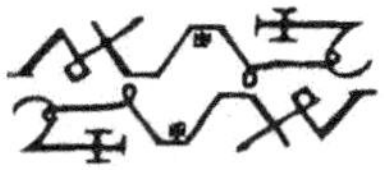

Michael.
Archangel Michael
Man - Michael Edward
Sunday 10th July 1994, 4.00am

Preface

The writings began in June 2020 and continued into early 2022. I was strongly encouraged to write them by Reverend Michelle Baum of North Shore Spiritualist Church Sydney NSW Australia.

Within two months I had written many prose poems. To begin with I was more interested in experimenting with writing under meditation.

At the end of 2020 I approached Michelle again to ask if I should continue. I was not sure what the writings meant and didn't see how they could serve any greater purpose. She asked me to take a break from writing them and read what I had written. There was a flow and pattern to the writing that often included the same subject two days in row. I could not remember the writings after I had recorded them and was amazed to observe the poetry turning into prose and developing into a journal of subliminal insights.

From that day forward I continued to sit for the meditations and I referred to what I wrote down as "The Writings"

One morning after doing my usual meditation and scrawling down what I had experienced I turned on mainstream TV. There on the screen was evidence of the same scenario I had just written about in poetic symbology. It was around the time Donald Trump president of the the USA was shaking hands with many of the other prime ministers and presidents from around the world.

So now I continued the writings as a way to confront the insanity of a planet falling into chaos. They also served to slow down my anxiety to survive the hardest part of the lock downs.

By mid 2020 people had become polarized in their opinions creating a huge immobilizing psyop of global grief and shock. For myself the effect of the lock downs were profound. I felt as though some subterranian monster had woven its way into our hearts and minds and cast us out of a land of plenty into a parallel universe controlled by inhumane forces. I became so isolated from the rest of humanity as I was unable to find common ground or get out to meet up with any other like minded souls in order to make sense of it all.

By late 2020 I felt I had no choice but to search for answers from my own meditations writings and research. I was deeply shocked by what I uncovered and what was not being discussed on the local and international mainstream news channels.

By the end of 2021 my TV broke down and I decided not to replace it. I had become genuinely traumatized by the fear mongering from mainstream media. It felt like a deliberate distraction especially as there never seemed to be any real reporting of what was actually happening at local community level. I vowed that even if the lock downs ended I would publish the writings as a record of my personal experience and share them to my website - jaynee.com.au

I started reciting some of them as audios on my Facebook page jaynee"Visions of my Life" as a weekly event but I didn't manage to keep that going regularly enough.

In May 2021 the first Kyogle Writers Festival was born. I became involved as a volunteer helping the street busking artists musicians and poets to recite their original work to a passing audience. As I had been a busker myself many years before I was comfortable in this role. I took the opportunity to present my most controversial poem using an old original music studio recording composed in 1992. The soundtrack suited the concept of the virus the vaccine the faces and corporations behind the pandemic and personified them as the return of Dracular. I performed "DracisBack"on Roxy Lane a side street in Kyogle designated for buskers. It immediately grabbed the attention of Andrew Spencer, a talented poet and writer with a publishing company called R.I.P. (Raised Ink Press).

Andrew invited me as a guest artist from the festival to do an interview on his radio show at River FM in Lismore. Kyogle and Lismore were beginning to thrive with new venues attracting a mecca of emerging and alternative artists and writers. From here I was inspired to transform DracisBack into a theatrical performance for the Nimbin Poetry World Cup and release it as a single with Gyro-stream on Spotify.

As part of the Festival of Words I also presented the second edition of my poetry book "Visions of a New Kind" first launched at Darwin fringe festival 2018. I took the opportunity to continue to exhibit my life size collage illustration to the poem "The Promise" at Kyogle Gallery.

"The Promise"and the short film called "Land of the Warthogs" helped me to become visible as a local artist in the Northern Rivers of NSW. The dream or vision that inspired "The Promise" happened before 1984. I could never have envisioned in my waking life back then that humanity would inherit the living nightmare we now find ourselves in. The uncanny accuracy of the images and symbols in that vision still haunt me to this day.

Almost twenty years on from 9/11 and the twin towers operation until now the new emerging alternative media have begun to expose many of the Agenda 21 conspiracy theories as conspiracy facts. The challenge of the collage painting was to throw those images on a the back of an old cupboard door rescued from the last Darwin cyclone as my chosen canvas. The collage is now the front cover of"The Writings"

Thanks to the photo shop expertise of Gail Faye mentioned in the acknowledgements The vision of "The Promise" described in poetry became a testament to the conception of "The Writings".

My other exhibit a short film called "Land of the Warthogs"had been my draw-card as an artist until now as it had been accepted for Melbourne Fringe Festival Victoria 2003. It was a dark allegorical fairy tale performed as a masked pantomime using subtitled spoken word poetry and a unique soundtrack composed by a talented artist from Edgecore productions Byron Bay. When I became aware of the disclosures thirty years later a parallel message also emerged from its depths. Finally I understood the childlike reference to an underworld of SRA (satanic ritual abuse).

In the 1990s when I created Warthogs as a soundtrack poem and film I had no knowledge of such things. My other creative achievement from the two years of superimposed personal retreat was "The Poets Breakfast". This was held once a month in my home town under the inspirational guidance of Vincent Stead a dedicated well known, well loved poet and chairman for North Coast Poetry and Spoken Word.

In the Northern Rivers poets breakfast events were held in different towns and we visited each others venues to celebrate our love of creative expression. I wanted to include my small town in this circuit to overcome feeling withdrawn and isolated. I became inspired to help my surrounding neighbourhood move beyond fear as I had done. It was a way to stay reconnected to each other and enjoy freedom of speech and self expression. Inevitably I read my writings at these local events which encouraged me to publish "The Writings".

19. 06. 2020

The overshadowing of a native
Indian man in an animal skull hat
A bird on some eggs
Which are the messages to be birthed
I can see through the nest
To how they are being laid
I have a headache
Slightly like sinus almost nauseous
My thinking is very foggy
Knocked out of normal alertness
I have a lump that feels
Like it's in my throat chakra
And there is ringing in my ears
All this can indicate
There are messages waiting for me
According to the training I have experienced
During many group meditations
Over twenty five years or more

20. 06. 2020

Hope and patience are not virtues anymore
But necessities
Our global paradigm is changing
Language is changing on the move
And more specific than ever
Life as we know it has changed
And morphed moving forwards
It is not enough to sit in a chair
And contemplate the change
We have to become it
Become a beacon of hope
And have patience that all will be revealed
As it should be
As above so below in due course
This paradigm shift on the planet
Is not man made
It calls upon the solar system to realign
A few people with ulterior motives
Cannot control all that
It requires immense effort and patience
Like an elephant lifting a big stick
Patience that humanity will get it in time
Not in time as we know it on the planet now
But in time we will all come to know it
And our forefathers before us will get it too
As indeed there is no time
It all morphs into the same time
The one reality
Hope is the essence of time
And we create time

Out of it springs our understanding
Of hope and patience
But in essence they are a construct
And we are moving in timelessness
Simultaneous timeless zone does not
Need to contemplate itself it just is
We don't have to have patience
When we are patience
Just as we don't have to have hope
When we are hope
So saying I speak to you in the now
Of all that is simultaneous
Till next time ... just joking

21. 06. 2020

The worm turns in the ground
Life comes around again
Purple maze of flowers in my face
Slowing down the pace of life
Life is not a race
Or an empty cardboard box in an empty room
While the worm turns in the ground
While the worm still turns in the ground
Peel back the banana or sugar cane on the field
Bring back your horse and plough
Increase your yield and eat
The farmer does not have to bite his lip
For the glossy printed paper money
Disappearing over time
While the worm turns in the ground
While the worm still turns in the ground
A Chinese man in a pointy hat is tilling his field
By hand with furrows in the dirt
We say thank you Yangtze

22. 06. 2020

Pale pain paddle your own canoe
Reuse what you know and have
Axe from middle ages and knights of old
Castles maidens myths strongholds
Worn out soles of the shoe
Walking through the mists of time
The maiden writes with a quill
And tells tales of torture from the tower
Behind thick walls and closed doors
She also flies like a bird with the feather in her hand
Freedom of the pen throughout antiquity
The pen as a sword of truth and not an instrument of deception
Pray blessed be they the whistle blowers the storytellers
They are truly the free and the brave
Whatever the idiom create the great moments
Within the movement of the scribes with pen or quill

29. 06. 2020

Bottle bagged couture perfumed
Based in an industry that favors glitz
Metal contamination in the new brand of medication
You can't ask questions
About potions made in laboratory stations
What is the world coming to says the old timer
Where is the world now says the youth
What is the point of industry passed
Where hand sanitizer poisons our hand
And contaminants from our
Products poison our land
Where vaccines are only designed to kill
Where the needle is a gun
That pierces your arm
And the medics are henchman
Employed to do harm

30. 06. 2020

Yasonite black woman skipping
Old mop and bucket washing the floor
She shines the bike light's sideways
Her family are coming through the door
Mama wears a headscarf
At a knot upon her brow
While steel girders are launching fabrications
Filling our minds and changing our laws
When the people speak out against slavery and servitude
When the system ceases to shoot us down in flames
When the military lay down their guns to end the game
The real grass roots people will rise again
To clap their hands and sing
The simple man will hold the match
To re-ignite our human life continuing
The shadows will be floodlit as if light had just turned on
Masonic walls will be dismantled brick by brick till they are gone

10. 07. 2020

Rabbit hole and a looking glass and lots of grass
Humanity and UFO flying over
Creating a patch of blue sky on a dark night
The broom with a green handle sits by the door
Near the mop and bucket ready to sweep things clean
But lying idle waiting while strange objects I cannot recognize
Versions of UFO technology to the simple eye
Mix and match headlights on a machine that could be a car
A guitar moulded out of chewing gum looks quite bizarre
Sometimes having a foot in a future we don't want
Is a way to work out how to change
What are we doing from where we are
Traumatized by the overloads of information makes it hard to look
The looking glass looks murky until you catch a spark
Or thread or line of thought to follow through
Then it all goes clear again and you can see the rabbit
In the field eating the green grass
And my carrots and other vegetables as it should and if I let it
But then the rabbit becomes ominous again
Like some robotic AI monster
Clanking tin version of reality have I been gas lit
What's the truth
I watched the roll out of tests and vaccines
In brown cardboard packages with red labels
Being distributed from the sides of white trucks
And I asked myself what is this charade all for
Vaccines and tests when the sky is clear
Where there is no pandemic lurking
Where the trucks are squeaky clean sterile and robotic
In plain sight under a blue sky and I ask-
Why did we agree to this as bystanders lurking close by

11. 07. 2020

So what is the answer and the solution I ask in my mind's eye
When the truth is right in front of us
But we cannot see it through our fear
The sky is clear the sky is clear
The rabbit is again signposting to its hole
There is some writing on a placard somewhere nearby where he stands
He is protesting alone and the public think he's mad
Like the Hatter and the tea party will soon come by to start again down the rabbit hole
The vicious cycle of an economy in wrong hands and he says we've all been had
His sign says: save the earth from falling down the hole
He's written it by hand in black and white and very bold
The helicopters and the drones have come to see
They fly over like giant insects that will not let me be
But still he writes in his calligraphy
About the petrol pumps and drought conspiracies
He is the necromancer of our times without the stopwatch in his waist coat
Because he is a rabbit after all eating grass and vegetables is where his destiny is at
Meanwhile we all exclaim what is that the chain reaction on a loop that faces back
Threatens to encase him in a rabbit prison
But it's not a prison for a rabbit who can burrow underground
It is a human prison in a field of fresh green grass
Alice is in Wonderland or looking through the glass
The solution is the potion that we are forced to drink
Is the potion the solution

If it changes how we live and how we think
We need to feel our feet up on the ground
To slow the murky mirror in our eyes
To stop the kaleidoscope of mirages and lies
To still the mind and calm the fears whipped up
To raise the fallen chalice and stand it up
The rabbit comes to look while munching carrots
We see the cup is still half full and grab it
As we can but choose to look at it this way
Then the rabbits and their annoying habits can go away

12. 07. 2020

Yoga swimming more yoga stretch the body
Doing somersaults off a flat diving board
Stretch your limbs to free your mind
Pay attention to your organs especially your throat
Microwave false teeth boogeyman eyes
Like scarecrows for animals in a field
Hook and line but not the sinker
Corner of the bathtub and corner of the house
Statue of Christ with a wooden hand
Statue of Liberty holding a flare
Man on a surfboard on a murky dark wave
Israeli women look out from a cage
Stately hallway but the carpet is blue
No statesman to talk and no audience too
The news as we know it has ceased to exist
Barnacles by the sea but where is the boat
The sea is still rising but we're not afloat
The water is clear as a windowpane
Because I'm safe in my house
While the world is alone

13. 07. 2020

Small antique wheel on the side of a cart cloaked in mist
Large parts of our family histories gone amiss
And upside down
And steel girders for a concrete foundation
A bowl of half eaten fruit lights up on a table
The cycles of life in the solar system as we know them
Cannot be depicted that easily on a 2D chart
There is a metal tower
That goes up into the sky and birds land on the top
And a man in a hard hat stands at the base
Constructions being made to go
Round corners not previously seen
An ancient photo copier on a rubbish bin
A cricket ball and a fisted glove
Is this all that remains of the ones we love
We change the meaning and the use of things over time
And the stories of our family genealogy
Become twisted to fit the narrative of the dominant few

14. 07. 2020

An antique child's pram comes into view
Baby is a china doll fragile and broken as the histories of fear inherited
An elaborate estate like a castle holds the poisoned apple
Not drowning yet but waving is the experiment of the elite and handshakes
How many waves before we all go under in submission to our fears inherited
The child grows up imprisoned inside the castle gates
Never knowing the outside world until too late
Breeding and bred to be aristocracy and elite
Is not a privilege but a prison also with no escape
The systems behind the systems we see
Many hands on a crystal ball manipulating the outcome
Underestimating the power of the universe to intervene
The child within the antique pram
Is a china doll that's broken
The authority to hand out stickers to control us
Has imploded down the rabbit hole
Which has become the outlet for a huge explosion
The earth is spewing up the contents of its inhumane nations
Don't be deluded into thinking
The plastic sticker is the only thing to save you
Out of the ruins of our ancient monuments only a chimney remains
Remnant of the aristocracy that once controlled us
The embers of the fire still glowing under a clear blue sky

17. 07. 2020

Arm is a limb to cushion the elbow
Hydraulic stump
Woven sunrise or sunset
A bird has a stick looking for a nest
A white sheep on a dark night is like a beacon
Strange things in the night move around
Where they walk we can't see them till sunrise
Meanwhile we feel them and still have to keep a healthy intention
We bandage our broken limbs that way
One day the new dawn comes up like a veil lifted just like that
We can breathe again and see what went bump in the night
A hairy caterpillar or possum is a different perception
The wolf suit that is a cape for human protection
The mask is no mask when it's no longer worn
The sheep are not such beacons
When they have been shorn

18. 07. 2020

Pipe feeding what part of the human drama
Drain with plug filtering storm water leaves
Hair curlers to dynamite
A crooked arm plays a cymbal like a reflecting light
A rear vision mirror for hindsight
A pedestrian crossing says stop slow down
To allow non automated life to survive out the ground
While the storm still brews in the trees
And a false leg off an amputee lies idle
An egg shoots out of a glass and into space
A child's toy that resembles a windmill
Goes down the stinking toilet
A pot boils on the stove and then milk spills out all over the place
To get wiped up again with a massive sponge
All those things that were done
With good intention
That have now become undone
Like an icy breeze blowing through a ships mast
That must now move forward as it can't undo the past
Otherwise the ship stops still and ghostly
On an otherwise deserted ocean
Like the ancient mariner died on board
So does the ship sink to the seabed
Or make its way like a floating graveyard onward to the shore

21. 07. 2020

The heirophant is upside down double speak
Political mayhem in Iraq, Iran and the Middle East
The flame from a gas-bottle does not have to blow up the bottle
One piece of the pie isn't even distribution of wealth to every nation
The light on an antique streetlamp is a chandelier in the night
Against a black night it can light the way
What divides the heart within the rib cage
Can become a lazar beam moment of truth
Like an astronaut in a suit about to walk
Out of the capsule surrounded by the universe
Who can still stay connected to his roots
Gas is only light when it is harnessed
And truth is only truth when it's not tarnished
Gas is still not light when it's not lit
And the earth has many treasures in its midst
Be still enough to listen and to pray
No single thief will take all that away

22. 07. 2020

Bent wire on a washing line blown by the wind as winter has come
The arches on the Sydney Opera House are like birds beaks waiting to be fed
The daffodils have fallen over in the vase and the mooring at the jetty has no boat
The corner of the book has blank pages while the dollar floats like a note on an invisible sea
From the corner of my eye I see the number 3
The internal workings of a deadlock not in place on the door
An old style car drives past a building somewhere in Cuba
The typical sombrero trio sing to an empty room and they remain upbeat
Never losing faith to keep performing in difficult times is quite a feat
Sometimes there's an alternative route on a dirt road around a troubled cluster of buildings
The road less traveled by the wealthy but well worn by the peasants who knew it
A caterpillar sandwiched between rich leaves peeps out at a new world
About to contemplate its metamorphosis
A rose in a dark room turns its head to the only window bringing light
The machine that makes the hay has started turning slowly
And the farmer tips his hat to the scarecrow in the field
Strange spotlights are beaming through a window on an object
On the bottom of a dungeon floor
A hiding place for a miniature robotic space module
Reflecting back to a world of technology growing fast in the high light of day

Streets are no longer recognizable the way we once saw streets in the olden days
I search for hope for humanity between the antiquated and the fantastic futuristic
Where the collision of these two worlds could be seen as an absurd way of looking at it
If parallel worlds not divided by time are all now coexisting at once

24. 07. 2020

A stick arrow on the ground points this way
As a thumbs up to where the grass is greener
The harpoon waits and aims at an unseen target
The hand that pulls the arrow back wears no glove
A hooded man in a full mask is half hidden in a doorway
Like some medieval battle being prepared in modern outfits
There are machines that I have never seen before
I have no idea what they would use them for
Adaptions from a scrap metal yard to fulfill a modern futuristic age
A stranger version of a faucet for the water pouring into metal basins
The wheel of an old fashioned cart trundles down a shingle road
Like images of steam punk art and the number three reverses to resemble om
Is this the symbol of the wave to come and if so will we return to horse and cart
And redesign our world from a colonial past to utilise the good old days for some new reason
I contemplate these things from my mountain hut in the winter season

25. 07. 2020

Matrix sheep or battering ram
Plane into a tower or just a fold in the invisible world
Is this 9/11 revisited or the incarceration of my mind
A street lamp like the moon on a stick is villainous illusion-ism
A dog with a plastic cone around its neck cannot see sideways
True vegetables cannot be made by sticking a card in a slot to open a door
The bandana around the neck of a fluffy poodle shows he is owned
The middle finger on the button that presses what elevator
And to where
I want to see real broccoli not reconstructed from metals in a boiling broth
Meanwhile manufacturing gobbles the raw materials
To force feed us on imitation byproducts
Like the artificial hand that guides real wood along the assembly line
A safety pin cannot hold the fabric of society together
An apple is an apple after all no matter the artificial hand that holds it
Or the mechanical spoon sending it to be slaughtered
The veins of a leaf under X-ray turn into a ballerina
Dancing perfectly rejoicing in the natural world
But now the X-ray glass has broken and the leaf is broken too
And falls from view after all it is only a perception
Of the natural world trapped under a microscope
London's Bridge and tower at twilight reflect a huge dark history in the UK
Or has my mind just turned to cauliflower my brain cooking itself with cheesy sauce
Spare me that thought while I think I have the illusion of flu

Until the veil is lifted on my foggy brain that is still attached to my head
I breathe a sigh of relief to awaken from all the madness and disorientation
Of thinking I am half human half machine
Mickey Mouse with red shoes on the ground is not of my creation
A scrambled brain is not the same with bacon
Wake up from this nightmare unchain your brain
The real moon is emerging from behind a cloud under a night sky
You can walk with real feet like I am
Empowered by knowing that we are still real and alive

26. 07. 2020

A farmhouse across from a green field
A creature with slanting black eyes is looking at me
A daisy keeps coming up on the lawn
A red roof on an American barn
The ears of a fox or is it a cat or a fox catsuit
Birds calling after the rain in real time
A tractor pulling a wheel to make hay bales
What do they say make hay while the sun shines
One day the truth will be out and the demon reduced to a creature
In a fox catsuit with black slanting eyes
Nothing to fear more than a monster in a child's story book
Would that scare you or not
Not as long as you dont look into its eyes

27. 07. 2020

Big dam gates are opening and water is draining out
There is a plug at the bottom to allow it to empty
As it empties I see two huge crocodiles
Looking at me smiling and wearing sunhats
Saying something like
We dont mind a bit of sun even though we are swamp creatures
Two rabbits are facing away from me
Holding a stick between them
Looks like they are trying to build something
Across the dam which is now a river
Now they have turned into beavers
And they look at me showing their long teeth

29. 07. 2020

Caterpillar crawls over a live match
Ground cover could include a four-leaf clover
A hand reaches up holding a cloud or is it cotton wool
The hand and arm change color like many races in one
There's a child's toy windmill I used to blow
At a sideshow at a circus when I was still innocent
As a child is supposed to be
We would blow all the colors into one
If I am to find a message of hope for humanity in this
It is about human solidarity
In the circus that is our world right now
We dont have to go into cold storage we can still have fun
While the events have to play out it seems
On our planets sideshow full of freaky masks and political clowns in a row
With their mouths open like puppets with nothing to say
All in a row waiting for the ball to drop in and they will say nothing till then
But in a child's mind at the circus sideshow we can chose what game we want to play
As a child knows who ever is in control we can choose to pay and play
So we rule the game that way as we know we are in control if we pay
Now I am seeing the burning hoop display that has turned into a tree growing leaves
Or a symbolic tree with leaves growing
Almost like a sculpture made in plasticine by human hands
Is it our future development plan
Now there's a yellow dirt road that goes in a straight line and disappears into the horizon

The path may not be smooth but it is fully visible ahead
At the moment there is no-one on it but I imagine crowds of real people
On foot will eventually find it like I have and start walking and talking as they do
Even the tiny insects will give their thumbs up when that happens
The huge claws of the tiger have dug into the ground in-front of me
I do not feel he is the enemy but rather holding the space and energy
A symbol of huge strength so I am not afraid
We may only be able to see what is in the corner of the window frame
Through the glass at the moment
But outside a picture is emerging if we stand back far enough and refocus
Maybe the rest of the image will come into view
This we can do from the safety of our houses
After all we are not expected to look beyond our own backyard
And not outside the gate just yet

30. 07. 2020

A white bell begins to ring at Christmas
A rainbow prism on a black and white sky
Checkerboard like the game of chess played with our lives
But there is a dove of peace very visible because of all of this
Like the holly beneath which we used to kiss
A man in a blue suit
The earth blowing up like a balloon from out of space
Food on the table to celebrate
While metal girders are being driven into the ground
With their waste like fallout shavings on the dirt
The birds still manage to sing on the wires
The man in the tinfoil hat takes it off
Because what was once conspiracy theory
Is now conspiracy fact

01. 08. 2020

Back end of an automated broomstick
Exhaust fumes funneled deliberately from the rear
A lawnmower with a funny top and a magpie in full dive
Looks at me from the corner of its eye
Rows of streets with houses all the same
On a never-ending cycle or revolution
Not my idea of home
A white glove is still a white glove under X ray
But it is pointing away from the glass
Farm machinery with attachments for making furrows
A massive wrench bolted on a dock
Is pulling up a mooring rope
For a paddle steamer or something huge
I am travelling back up through a hole in the ground
Like a worm coming to the surface
After hibernation I have been waiting for a clear sky
And now drawn to the rays of the sun I am moving up
Many creatures throughout earths history have done the same
Hiding in natural monuments to antiquity
Until the time is right but not restricted by time
Cycles of life and creatures that have created
Structures as we have known them
Even when we dont they exist as evidence

02. 08. 2020

Dingo looking through a broken wooden fence
A slice of pizza from which a mandala springs
From something ugly to a grandiose design
If you zoom out and refocus it becomes like a design
Embedded in old architecture on the ceiling of a dome
Ornate and eastern in appearance
The dingo spies a rabbit in the grass
Behind the fence that is like a cage
Just as ornate as the ceiling that could also be in Rome
It's coming back into view so does the contrast
Epitomize the need for freedom behind the corruption
Of the structures that enclose us that prevent us from
Following our natural instincts
The rabbit is the only creature that seems free
The grass is greener on its side of the fence
But how did it get in there
A hand comes up to break apart the broken fence
The same hand behind the building
Of the ancient architectural dome and place of worship
To the dingo it is a giant human hand
To the worshiper it is the hand of God
But it all depends on your situation
Or how trapped you feel in that
Which colors your perception
Strangely now the bunny rabbit has
Ceased to be natural and has just joined a sideshow
Riding a dodgem car with fake rabbit ears
It was the unrestricted freedom of the green grass
The choice to be free was what the dingo really wanted
Not the rabbit after all

03. 08. 2020

Posies of flowers promise to brighten days to come
Cobra dances from the box in trance while the Indian man plays the flute
The lid on a garbage bin or sewer is turning
It is a plastic lid on concrete base
There is an old fan blowing on the ceiling of a bunker
I hear the birds sing in real time outside my window
And it lifts my thoughts out of world war and the like
My spirit sings too remembering the coming
Out of the winter of devastation that marked the last world war
This war is different but it triggers my memory of the last one
Something in my DNA remembers food on the table that is healthy in real time
Makes me want to paint a picture of it like a precious memory
A gift from the universe coming out of the drab draconian
Lock down into a vibrancy where the simple pleasures are magnificent moments in time
How must the cobra feel at the music of the snake charmer
Released from its prison looking back down a plughole from the top
Where you can see where everything is going
That is another whole perception to being down the plughole
An Indian man makes his living
In the backstreets but they are all empty at the moment
Only the duty bound once whitewashed walls and the uneven pathway beneath his feet
Like echo chambers to the absence of people
Who normally fill every square inch of the walls and pavement with vibrancy
Then I see the banner is waving again like multi-maroon strips of cloth on a pole
To signal the end of the end

05. 08. 2020

Underbelly of a flying saucer silhouetted against the hill
With colorful crowds of people on its summit
Gathered for that reason underneath
The ship is hovering with its underbelly unlit
Like it is waiting also but we are aware of each other
Piece of string between two metal clamps
Says that we can define how long that piece of string is now
There is no fear of alien invasion or takeover
Just because the ship is huge and more advanced in technology
We will have to grow in consciousness
Before we know how to switch the lights on however
To communicate fully and see beyond the fear mongering
That tells us it's for our own benefit to shoot
The ship from the sky
They are only our neighbors come to help
And the enemy is within the earth
A posy of flowers over the lock on a shut window
With a cyclone outside
Suddenly the lock and window
Are shattered to reveal a whole new world
Post apocalypse of a different kind
Strange edifices I cannot recognize
Made of some metal and unknown substances
I guess they are robotic
And there is a flying disc lowering itself to the ground
Not such an unexplained phenomena anymore
It seems as if it is in plain sight
Twilight zones of our past re-emerge in my memory
Depictions of love shaped light beams from an unknown source

Somewhere in the sky in black and white
Then I see a whole different concept of a lighthouse
On a cliff to warn seafarers about the shore
Something we romanticized once is not romantic now
And could be menacing if you didn't understand
How it worked or what it was for

11. 08. 2020

Mum and birthday candles
As a crack in the corner of the house
Lets the light in and reveals
The old bullock in the field
My mother as a young girl
With a head full of ribbons
And tongue in groove walls
Camelias in a posy of flowers
And my mother holding a
Golden key to something
The old paper we used to
Dress up a birthday cake with
Comes into view to celebrate
She is saying celebrate
The goose that lays the golden egg
Is not in what you own or you borrow
But in what you squirreled away
In a small safety deposit box
It may be simple and humble
But it is the key to your freedom
As only time will tell
I'm saying to her
Thank you Mum you have remained
Very wise in the face of adversity
Very patient with your most rebellious child
Yet also but for my journey in life
I would never have come around
To this point of view
But for the survival of my ancestors
Through adversity
Encoded in my genes
Like a memory inherited
I would never have known what to do now

19. 08. 2020

When we are grieving for the ones that we shared
Happy times with and that we love
It's like old memories and precious antiques
They come back in bits and pieces broken up emotionally
Meanwhile our pen has dried out and the sideshow sign has fallen down
And all the clowns are laughing sideways as our memories turn to vapor
And disappear through the hole at the top of an old fashioned key
Like the memories of when pegs were still wooden
When we hung our clothes out to dry made from natural fibre and precious
The wingnut beneath the bolt has come loose but the horse hasn't bolted
He turns around and looks at me because I left the stable door open
He looks at me as if to say it's open
He is a big draft horse with hairy legs and a bemused expression
It doesn't compensate for the pain that he is still here
But it makes me feel better to think that all is not completely gone and lost
While he is still blocking the exit

20. 08. 2020

Welcome dear one for we are united beyond time
But trying to recreate the time machinery artificially
Is to play Russian roulette with your life
And often causes your passing
You have always known you can step into the future
As you do it many times in your sleep
What you recreate in your waking life as human beings is *but a reflection of the bigger picture*

Note to myself:
Look through the window
You can do it from your fireside anytime that you feel confused or out of your depth
Ask for Michael's sword to cut through the illusion to bring you back to the truth and the earth where you can always remain grounded
Like the sword points to the ground to earth you with its blade touching the earth hold each side of the handle to give you strength

21. 08. 2020

A rose is a gift of peace as well as love in the shadow of the man
In the suit with his back turned right in front of me
It turns from red to pink like an X-ray that shines through his heart
He could be from another era as his suit has padded shoulders
And he wears a dark hat with a stature that is very intimidating from the back
But he is here to tell you all is not lost in this game we are forced to play
The eye of Osiris is upon us but it has come to herald a new day
If I was to look at the statue of liberty from underneath
It would be as if an umbrella had opened out to shield the sun
The death of the old world has been very sad
But the man is not broken as a new day has just begun
As I held the rose up to the fence it still had buds
But began to change from the original red
Meanwhile a paintbrush is whitewashing the wall
And my mind spins around now upside down in free fall
It makes me dizzy but I now see the man in silhouette
Has come to set humanity free after all the changes that have now begun
Unraveling before him in the setting sun
He is a lonely figure but he is not alone
As there is another figure from an Arabic country
Dressed in white on the other side of all that must be done tonight

22. 08. 2020

Someone significant has died as I see flowers and a coffin
D.T. is standing there in silence honoring this person
And the marking of this occasion
As a hand holds a vessel made from delicate porcelain
Opaque in the shape of an eggshell half
A peacock walks with tail feathers down
There is a two seated Indian style chair floating above the water
The water is rising and there is a wheelchair also exiting the scene
There is a symbol of a white arm brandishing a stick like a weapon
Above a sea of people there is a trophy on a table
Of a strange flying creature that turns into a black machine
Then it becomes a close-up image of a blow fly
From underneath flying the wrong way up
Someone is behind a piano in a humble barroom
And I can see the black shoes of a dead person
They are singing about them but I only see the back of the piano
There is a thin and bloodied hand holding onto a rail for support
Someone who feels desperate to cling onto life
The fuel rods of a jet as black hawks are being stacked ready for flight
A celebration across the sky is being prepared
Is it the military displaying its power
I am coming back to earth standing behind a mirror
Facing away from me attached to it is the bust of an identity
Whose power is destined to be remembered in between all these events
There is someone driving a vehicle who looks towards me
There is no passenger seat but even so they have asked me to hop in
Where the passenger seat should have been

There is a med bed like a solarium lit from underneath
It comes from another time
And once I lie on it I am transported to another time
Where huge creatures like dinosaurs are staring at me with lit up eyes
I guess that means they are nocturnal
And I'm not so sure this was a good idea to get in the car and lie on the solarium
As they say dont get in a car with strangers and the other bit about the bed you lie in
But he seemed so totally confident as if he knew where he was driving
And the bed instead of a seat looked too enticing
I could have said no but curiosity got to me or something
Now I want to go home and now I'm home again just like that
But I can return here to the no seat with the same driver anytime I like because it's a time machine
Maybe next time I will be more clear about where I want to go

Note:
I see the silhouette of a person with long hair on a seat to my right who has a halo of gold above their head and they say the halo came from time travel but we have forgotten its symbology. The ancient masters of past and future have used it to travel throughout time for eons witnessing events that human consciousness has not arrived at yet to understand
Arrival is a state of consciousness beyond time we do not have to die to achieve it. It is a state of consciousness that transcends time as we know it. That has been as naturally occurring as a koala eating gum leaves and as it was a part of our inheritance it was stolen.

24. 08. 2020

Teapot to Aladdin's lamp
The conversation that will work miracles
An ox with huge horns tills the fields in India
People go about their business
Mothers in saris and babies on their backs
The hustle and bustle of life is coming back
The earth moving equipment that
Tried to flatten the beauty of natural life
Was an unsuccessful clumsy attempt
While the miracle of life springs back
Not even in retaliation
But in its simple and profound
Magic of regeneration
A posy of flowers once again
Showing the good that has sprung out of adversity
And just because we took the time
To have a cup of tea and a chat with our neighbors
All over the world
We called upon the genie in the lamp
To rescue us from adversity
Did Edison really invent the light globe
At the beginning of a revolution
That ended in an atom bomb
Can we now shed light
On the dark untruths about our human history
While the true narrative remains undisclosed
What manipulation over centuries
When the truth is the only light
That cannot be extinguished
Once the genie emerges from the lamp
The darkest corners will be floodlit
The cap on the extent of that disclosure

Has already been half removed
Honestly the sun could be a doughnut
If you look at the light around it
And imagine its centre to be a hole
So the tinpot conspiracy theorists
Have something to say
But not until the cap on knowledge
Is fully removed will it all make sense
When will we get the whole picture
And not have to play guessing games
With half the puzzle pieces
By then the all seeing eye of Horus and Osiris
Will be visible in the sky
And the chariots of fire
Will again be present on the earth
So raise your frequency little ones
As the swords have crossed
Not in battle but in truce
The fate of your cities is safe in a much bigger hand
When the flags of your nations
Are at a world ceremony
The true kingdom can now open its gates out
And all our mythologies can be realigned
To be examined under a floodlight redesigning
The future of humanity not through a microscope
But on a large light box on a table lit
Also from above with a massive ceiling lamp
No longer confined to the ether with the spiders webs
And the folk law throughout the ages of human history
The genie is out of the lamp and the game is over

26. 08. 2020

Elephant ivory symbolic and a smiley icon from an online chat
A volcano erupts into a hockey stick graph and becomes a broken leg on a Santa sleigh
Symbolic of broken promises by Xmas and an unfulfilled dream as Santa is grounded
A pygmy African appears or is he Amazonian
He is carrying wood or bamboo poles on his back
They open out like a fan as he looks at me trying to tell me something
The mouth of a woman opens and out of it comes missiles
And other flying machines of war
An indigenous chain gang of people are bringing sticks out of a white hangar like a tent in single file
The knife goes back into the scabbard block but it is already bloodied
As poor people visit the graves of their dead in the middle of the night
Meanwhile a huge UFO covers the sky and I can see the workings from underneath
There is a metal star with a lazar beam at its centre point
From here the light comes out and floodlights the ground
So then I can see many lights under the craft
And a hand that looks gloved or automated comes out of the lights but it is not menacing
It feels alien or robotic even if it has five fingers and it seems to be here to intervene
For those who are oppressed and need it
Now I see maybe five lights inside their own spinning disc
One spin goes clockwise and the other anti-clockwise like antimatter suspension

There are illuminated creatures like insects and animals I dont recognize as from earth
They are coming out of the sides of the openings and
I'm being shown this like a mirror image back-to-back
To explain the mechanics of the technology if there is such a thing as a retro UFO this is it
Now I see arches and pillars of another civilization that left our planet a very long time ago
That continued as a civilization on another planet
It's all a bit Star Wars mixed with earlier scifi like Flash Gordon era
I'm back to the Christmas on hold image and a house window with lights on
It is surrounded by a wreath of holly in snow and a child's stick figure
Walking in an old-fashioned space suit
Air conditioning ducting looks like someone floating in space in a deep sea divers suit
The air conditioning pipe turns into a good old fashioned ceiling fan
Not sure where this is going
Nothing much allowed out in public at the moment so anything could be in the pipeline
We are cut loose from our information sources forced to turn inwards for guidance
Sputniks in space suits set adrift like the Bowie song Major Tom
Will we steer our ship with an old fashioned steering wheel
And a compass to tell us North South East and West in space
Or will we have to find a whole new framework to define our position in space
In this new era there's a space race and a space force but on earth the COVID vaccine
Has the human race been left in the dark very confused poor us

01. 09. 2020

Sickle moon mounted like an ornament and a hatchling of chickens in a star shape
As they have hatched
A hook beneath the ocean is rusted in the murky water
Shooting stars that look cylindrical asteroids with 5G cylinders stuck to them
The wheel turns on a child's toy blown by the wind
The grass has grown longer fresh and green by my garden hose
The change we have been waiting for has already started
My heart is with Uluru and Uluru is the heart
I see small wheels and tent guide ropes in my life and in my meditations
Because things are beginning to move soon we will be on the journey back
To the mother of all mothers when the Pleidian gate way hovers over the rock
The light of all lights will be switching on the natural magnetic grid
To re-balance the earth leaving 5 G and all these man-made artefacts
And their satellites for dead

04. 09. 2020

Thinking people in silence is like a cancer that grows as the grass grows
The tent poles fall over and there is a parachute
Waiting to rescue our thinking
And end an icon from byzantine times
Whose face glows with the gold halo
Encrusted into the mosaic
And then it turns into a clock face
Saying twenty to six or seven
I'm aware of the blue patch of sky in between the clouds
And a vehicle backing out of an automated garage
That also looks like a tent
It is a racing car backing out of its garage
In the sky racing against time put out by the universe
As a gift to help us to hit the accelerator
Fast enough for the time when things will speed up
And out of our control
A hand is holding up a small gadget
Between fore finger and thumb
Is it some mini computer too big for a nano chip
It's visible to the light of day
The blue sky behind the hand
Indicates it's a gift to help us on our way
Something that could be a branding iron of hot metal
Has just become suspended between two rods by an axle
I am transported back to the tiger moth aeroplane from WW2
And the amazing idea that the person in the cockpit
Is flying by winding up a rubber band
Early twentieth century technology- easier to fix
He is waving as the plane is turning towards me

With its one rotor blade on the front
Those magnificent men in their flying machines
Captain Baron Trump and the Bloody Red Baron
The old story written that has its parallel in Trump
Trumps son is a time traveller
Yesterday I couldn't let myself go under
For reasons I thought I needed to stay away from politics
But the first words in my head were
Where's the Trump factor what is this and is it a mystery
Or is he the other side of a mask
Being presented to humanity
With which to play out this battle
Of our values and beliefs about good and evil
Or the law of opposites from which we learn

09. 09. 2020

A blind comes out of the side of a house
And it is a black shield
It pulls out of a wall like a shade cloth
Of some kind to create another wall
New solar conductor invented or a 5 G shield
As a black rod that concertinas out of the soil
Like a lightning rod or another electricity conductor
Guttering made of see through plastic
Where we can watch the water flow
What is it that we need to know
What is it that we need to grow
Into as a society in our modern cities
Reconstructed on a grid that is not man made
But utilises the force of nature as it should
A smart city or town that is not controlled
Or a smart village in the surrounding ground
All self sustainable in a few short hops
No need to control a population
That can sustain itself to grow its crops
As we lay aside the New World Order
Which is the Old World Order after all
We can finally see what has been denied to us all
Once the war is won the bamboozling will stop
Humankind will find its solution in one small hop
Not a giant leap for mankind as we once thought
The black faced clown with painted lips
Is being washed by the rain and the mask has slipped
Beneath the dark prediction
A flower emerges from a spiral in space
I think it is a chrysanthemum in the pink

Symbol of a world emerging out of the darkness
Into a new solution for the human race
The draft horses pull a double cart
That is covered in a rusty red tarp
The contents of the cart hold some household items
That are very simple and very high tech
The solutions have been with us a very long time
Humanity had to slow down to see it and now it's around

13. 09. 2020

So what is the matter with Mary Jane ... rice pudding again
World War Three depression food shortages
And huge shelves to the roof with nothing on them
When growing your own food in a depression
Even dandelion weed tastes good if it is served and cooked
With the heart of good intention
Lily ponds and frogs in the garden
Supply trucks with labels on their sides but they are empty and the signs are old
Growing our own food starts with a stick in the ground
It turns into a blood red rose with two roses on the stick
Branching out in two directions
Two ways to go with our food in future
From a rose to a glasshouse in horticultural science
Two ways to grow food in the future from a seed to a weed
The ballerina is dancing as she looks out to sea
The dance is specific to set us all free
The new horizon can be reached even from a cage
If we pray the right way and stay in the joy of alignment
She is striking a particular pose
It is symbolic of a new freedom for our youth
And for the eternity of human consciousness
The continued hope for the human spirit
Now she is moving one leg out and begins to pirouette
On the one that remains on the ground
It is about balance in motion and the energy
That that movement creates in our lives
Now she is looking at me and bowing
Her hands in prayer position to acknowledge my presence
And show reverence to a fellow human being

17. 09. 2020

Obtuse angle for building specifications
Analogue clock at 10 am has red hands
Empty shopping carts
In a bubble and a car seat with no driver
A hamburger with a meat pattie
That could be real but could be 3D printed
A page of writing with an old fashioned ink pen
Today was multilayered so I couldn't write
On anything specific.
While it was still forming

18. 09. 2020

Thumbs up goes the cartoon character with a big fat hand
There's a broken window many floors up on a skyscraper
There's a leaking pipe that needs re welding
The millipede is curling its tail hanging from the green branch
The cartoon man is back
I see his face has a funny handlebar moustache
Something is coming out of the side
Of what could be a spaceship
All 3D printed construction with surveillance
A plinth on a Roman or Greek temple
Door frame and a metal towel rail
There is a lot going on but it is fragmented
And nothing is coming together as yet
Scattered but with some hope
For the future like there is an alternative plan
But I need my reading glasses
Meanwhile I take refuge in this funny little town

19. 09. 2020

Another posy this time all over type of flower
With a strong scent called Daphne again
The smell stays a long time
And there is a feeling of a funeral behind it
But the scent is overpowering and uplifting
There is a pixie in a hat doing push ups on a bar
Lift ourselves up by Christmas with an effort
The cogs in a big old wheel are turning
The rooster isn't crowing yet but he
Has lifted his head to show his bright colors
A fan turns into an old aeroplane propeller
At the front of a plane the Red Baron is back
Old fashioned power poles from underneath
Turn into a lighthouse with red and white stripes
An image of Trumps face dissolves into a white blob of paint
I am looking up at a canopy
And my clothes line from underneath
A caterpillar is trying to climb onto the top
There is a sense of climbing up to greater heights
A big feat for a caterpillar
With the promise of a butterfly to come
Still looking for a place to hang for metamorphosis
I am on the moon but I am hanging a horse blanket
And bridle over a rack
Symbolic of two states of consciousness
And time re emerging at once
Two different points
In technological development coinciding at once
Enveloped in the radiant energy
Of moonlight and something about

Hanging up your bridle and reigns
In ceremony and in plain sight
There are much bigger forces
At play within the magnetic pull
Between the earth and the moon
And that will manifest on the earth
To cause new creatures in the soil
And green leaves that have different vein structures
There will be a kink in the journey
To the top of the canopy but that is all
The caterpillar will get there

21. 09. 2020

I smell fragrances in spring
But are they from this world or another one
The colors of life become important to keep my energy up
I am surrounding myself with the energy
Of my friends who have passed
As though they are present in some form
It gives me comfort and strength
To remember them through the things they have left behind
Not to idolize them but to
Acknowledge their influence in my life
And how it has led to where I find myself today as a result
Such good people and such a blessing
That is too often overlooked or misinterpreted
By those of us still living on this planet
The beauty and reverence of our friendships
That abide with us beyond death
Is to be celebrated and remembered
Not altered by time but held in the gentle
Hands of timelessness
It takes us awhile to get there
While the hands of the time tick on
But eventually we find our resting space
And there we find our friends forever
Timeless friendship is so sweet
Fur black rabbit pops up and look at me it has been
Cloaked so I couldn't see it at first
It is a real rabbit but bits of machinery are trying to fit
Someone clamps two rocks together in their hands
And sets up a radiant vibration
Affecting the sun in that its a huge energy generated
Part of a face of a rock and a byzantine image
Of an angel descending
Removing it's self from a stained glass window

22. 09. 2020

There is a wreath HMS something Al and these events
Was there another story behind the story told
How dark must it get beneath
The ocean of human consciousness
Before we are willing to bring these things
Up to the surface out of the depths and into the light
There is a hand on a door handle saying
Once you know you don't have to go
Down the rabbit hole twice to uncover the truth
That humanity has been lied to
While living in an illusion and a bubble on the surface
But when you have been to the depths
And back you realize how we became manipulated
By fear and depravity many eons ago
Cut off from the waist down in our light bodies
Or cut off from the waist up
It seems surely the gut feelings that know
Something is wrong with the narrative
Is where we must start to rescue ourselves from
We are all composed of light and dark
Once we know this about ourselves
It is just a matter of bringing ourselves
Back into the light body connected
Trauma and abuse that we remember
From this life or another one
Doesn't have to be a negative trigger
But a call to stand back up and be in our own power
Once we have done it
Then we have an opportunity to be
More compassionately aware

Of the journey others will have to make
To reconcile their own soul with the truth
This way the darkness will come up naturally
And the demons of the past
Being recreated in this time
Can be finally cast out
And back into the past millennium
Of the human story

28. 09. 2020

The moon is an orange in the sky
Now three are two
With helicopter blades on them
To keep them hovering
Even though my lemon and orange tree is grafted
It still has a beautiful scent when it is in blossom
The sprout on a leaf turns
Into a sprinkler to water my plants
It is not the clone that is created
That creates the problem
But the mind of the creator that invented the clone
If it is not infused with love then it causes pain
It is the motive behind an artificial world
That brings about the destruction
Nature can adapt to many things
Which is the wonder and beauty of nature
Yet if we leave her
In her original form not manipulated
She is magnificent beyond worlds
So why do we want to settle for second best
When the original creator
Can take our breath away so completely
This way at least we can die happy and fulfilled

29. 09. 2020

A storm water drain with muddy water just sits
I look up through a stained glass table top
At the trees in a cultured garden
It is the breakfast room from days gone by
Where top hats and suits and gentlemen courted ladies
Things we call a thing of the past
Are still practiced in the courts
Of the elites when they are on display
Their days are bright and nights are dark
And full of ominous hidden secrets
The drain is back but now it's gushing after the storm
And sits sideways under a small stone bridge
It is flushing out the dark corners of the bedrooms
And the sewers of human degradation
A piece of round wood in a brace comes into view
It is the handle of an oar attached to a boat
A place to get away onto a lake
With frogs and lily pond leaves
There is a pine tree lit by moonlight
Alongside a path that feels like a lonely walk
In the park or something more sinister
Something in a green jar resembling a grasshopper caught
That turns into the pincers of a crab or crayfish or lobster
I am back at the tinny fishing at night
There are gold bars being created from a machine
I thought the lobster was smoking
Till I realized I was looking
At someone on a jetty in an old fashioned boat
A hat and pinstriped striped suit
Luxury symbols of the entitled

Some Earl from British aristocracy in days gone by
Or a traditional descendant a window into a privileged life
That appears oblivious toward the imbalance
And destruction being wrought upon the earth

01. 10. 2020

20° obtuse angle and puss from that side rises to the surface
Things are being measured through a protractor
That tries to order the natural world
In some way to control it
But the natural world just keeps growing
And doing its thing anyway
The person with the protractor
Is holding it up against a window
But they're inside trying to understand
How to control the outside like an autistic child
Brilliant but obsessed with angles and protractors
Locked away in their own version of reality
They cannot be part of the outside
Because of a genetic mutation
Forced to be locked up measuring a different reality
Driven by an unforeseen force within
Passionate about what we do not understand
There is a city out there that has been made
From the vision of the autistic child
All rubber and plastic and superimposed upon
There is an Indian man and a physician who has been around
Who has been aware of the agenda
And the process toward smart cities
He is from an oriental place
Where the mosques and temples still exist in their true form
His energy is a sigh of relief
As he helps to make sense of the two worlds
For the autistic child and for us
Forced to live in this unnatural reality
Mathematical calculations from a computer screen

Another Indian man with a white beard
Is speaking with a lilt and he
Unravels the mathematical calculations
In his speech the word matrix has an X at the end
Which is the crossover point
Between construction and deconstruction
It sits at the end of a structure to mark the spot
The tipping point from where things
Can become balanced and re balanced
The crew outside my window is suddenly very loud
Bossy smaller birds in flocks
Or are they complaining about the interference in larger bird domains
They seem unafraid of bigger birds
I have yet to understand the dynamics
Of natural bird flock relationships
According to the natural laws of flight and space

02.10.2020

The peacock is displaying itself at me in the shade of a tree
He is in the foreground
Silhouetted against a farmhouse with a red roof in the distance
Across from a long wide paddock of golden green grass
I see a child's tricycle handles of the old-fashioned metal variety
On the corner of a park bench seat
Someone has a strange looking lawnmower
That turns into a tractor of sorts
Suddenly lots of odd bits of farm machinery appear
I see the leaves on a vine
And bubbles coming to the surface of a pond
Something is at the bottom
Of the pond in a box
Is Dick Tracy trying to solve a murder
Last night he turned up in my meditation
Under the streetlamp a spotlight on his profile
Someone has their hand out
They are receiving what looks like a rock
Maybe precious uncut metal
It is a male hand that is either younger
Or not roughened by hard labour
It is the square of a taller thick set person
A seahorse could be in a fish tank
The coiled tail is significant

04. 10. 2020

Reactivating the crystalline grid
A crystal comes into view huge and opaque
Aboriginal women acknowledge
The tuning into Uluru switching on
After this smudging and raising frequency
Part of heart solar plexus
And akashic records in the sixth chakra
Uriel is purple for that reason
The vibration is also deep to go into earth
Celebrate with American Indians in full headdress
A doll in centre of the circle could be Amazonian
An amethyst crystal is cleansing the inner core
To bring all to the surface to be healed
Evidence of other planets like earth not to preclude
The abandonment of this one
Burning petrol stations not burning fossil fuels
Dark glasses to shield from atomic radiation
Is not the answer either
Confine the motor cars to track and sport day
While the rest of us gain our wings
Into a new true millennium not through mind control
I thanked spirit and the aboriginal women
And a hand rock symbol came up
Like a high five or a hand painted on a rock

05. 10. 2020

I see flames on the rock as though it is very hot
A plane appears from the centre of a black cloud
A black hole disguises time travel
Hands hold a rock with the face
Of a painting of Edward Munch The Scream
Shock and anxiety of the human condition
A UFO appears in plain sight
There are markings on the ground like Nazca lines in Peru
The underside of an ordinary rocket
Fuel based taking off from the ground
The UFO hovering very close to the centre part of the magnetic grid
My heart is in my mouth beating fast
Not with fear but vibration or anticipation
They're showing directed energy can work
From one cloud to another
There is a red dust around the rock
To disguise the UFOs flying through it
There is a sense of relief at having this kind of intervention
Uluru has many secrets
There is more to the story of Wolf Clan Dog Star
And humankind than the first race will tell us
Is it about a dog star or am I querying spirit
They are marking a point in time drawing a line in the sand
When enough is enough and humanity will have to wake up

06. 10. 2020

A fairy tale city with spires and aqua blue at each peak
A scroll unwinds like a cartoon edit
And I see Disneyland
To think all that innocent glitz would hide a pile of maggots
Being cultivated in a bucket
There is a flower spreading across a pond
But it doesn't look like a pond plant
It could be an acacia bush that hides the water source
There is a rose hidden on the underside
Of old world industrial machinery
Underneath the cog things are not as they seem
But there is a silver lining
And a promise of protection
For the natural world for all her adaptability
Is a blessing that will prevail
The industrial age and the machine
Has now turned into a giant water wheel
Maybe a paddle steamer
These things can still help us navigate
Our way out of turbulent times into calmer safer waters

09. 10. 2020

Dusty old green bottle painted
Into a still life on a table
But the apples are bright
So the opportunities are still there
For those whose lives have frozen
And become distant memories otherwise
We can still find ways to paint a new picture
From an old one
The apples remain brighter by contrast
The rest of the picture covered in cobwebs
The old life continues to fade
But opportunities that can be transformed
Are not missed
While dusty memories continue to fade
Into the mists of time and distance
Or get recycled into another life
They take on a whole new meaning
Second hand to many hands for someone else
Down the chain of human experience
As we move on
Genie in a bottle
Potions in liquid what's the outcome
Crystals formed by intent
Grass frozen in the ice all things frozen again
But not for too long
All goes rotten in the new spring
Yet much brighter days are coming
For those who have the intent
Where the soul can be happy again
After the winter of our discontent

12. 10. 2020

Telecommute wires come out of a wall
Like claws grabbing a light globe
A big digger earth moving machine
Has a grabber too that looks like teeth
A cockroach is irritated in unnatural soil
And the leaf that comes out of the ground
Is digitized with a bar code or mini chip
None of us want to live like that
Completely automated in a desert
With forces that are pushing us that way
They will eventually implode upon themselves
And move on from this planet
Leaving whatever independent life force is left
That is not controlled by artificial intelligence
As it does not serve their ultimate purpose
But to implode upon themselves
There is another way that requires humanity to grow up
Beginning with waking up and taking back control
The race is on whether you call it evil against life
However you translate it we need
To move beyond the paradigm
Counter propaganda alone cannot drain the swamp
When the creature is in our head

13. 10. 2020

Really strong energy after a smoking ceremony
Dreamed of Trump all last night
Mum was here today and yesterday
Crystal formation snow or ice crystalline grids
Space station satellites
Something leaves the station at warp speed
Pouring blood and water into a cavern
Transfusion as a lily among stock flowers
A screwdriver from underneath
Or a very strange tower coming out of a spiral
Trumps face looks intense as he is fully focused
On the war on humanity
The veil is about to be lifted
On who and what and who he is
Family lineage and the job to do from ancient times
Some people in a lifeboat
Looking at a cavern in a rock face with a light behind it
Dwarfing the size of the boat
A triangle lights up in neon in the sky
And has turned into a jet of some kind but white
Not a black hawk at the solar eclipse
There is something coming from the sun
Directed energy coming straight at my eyes
A hand is writing through a metal tube
Onto parchment or a scroll but in ink
Magna Carta of human rights
And a fushia bush in bud or are they berries
Tweedledum and dee cartoon appears
But mostly just the stomach
A version of a looking glass

To see to the other side of crazy events
It is a calm landscape a sea or lake on the other side
Meanwhile I see a crater
On another planet moon or Mars
A whole fleet of UFOs just came into view
In formation moving in the distance
With the largest one closest to me
As they are here

19. 10. 2020

A string on the forefinger
Puppets being pointed in a direction attached by strings
Freedom is not freedom with strings attached
Or promises of a package false advertising
In an empty cardboard box previously opened
With the contents removed
We are being stolen from before our very eyes
Forced by an unseen hand with empty promises
When it is we who will be put in the package
Marketed and sent off in a cardboard box
How do we avoid this I am asking
I am on public transport driving over the harbor bridge
At fast pace looking at an ocean
Through the bridge framework
How do we reconstruct the bridge
To be open and light and not in a hurry
To carry us over to new places at our own speed
I see cantilevers over the bridge
Showing me the structure is strong from the outside
A swing bridge with a winch to wind it in
The strings that once bound us
We can use to pull things out of the ocean
Or stump the anchor to the boat above it
Humanity can find ways to cross
What appears to be calm waters
Even ones that run deep
With hidden agendas beneath
We don't have to dredge the ocean
And start again to remove the dangers
When we already have the structures

Inventions overtime to help us out above deep water
It is about taking the restrictions off the structures
So they can work properly again
As they were designed to do
Before they became part of the elite master plan
Before that time was the universal plan
Always guiding us alongside
The evil intent of a few to control it
All this is just a moment in time
If we focus beyond the restriction
The fear of the strings
And the finger that points us
Into the cardboard box
To be sold as an item to be manufactured
We will see how magnificent
Our man made universe is once again
So humanity think outside of the box

20. 10. 2020

Daffodils fall out of a brown paper bag
Dropped on the pavement
August has come and gone
And the sun has become very piercing
As it begins to move in over the earth
Where there is a lack of ozone
Not from climate change but electromagnetic frequencies
As satellites break the ozone down
Political promises are laid waste
In the coming of an ancient prophecy
That was spoken of by traditional cultures
A totem pole has wings
As many things have come to pass
Where the clouds partially block the moon
On an otherwise bright night
The stuff of ghosts goblins
During Halloween
Or the uncovering of that myth and narrative
There are new structures appearing
Out of the fog in daytime
There is a plane showing its jet propeller
As things are afoot but not in the way we think
Behind the iron curtain once over Russia
Which is now Chinas globalist deep state

21.10.2020

Sweeping clean the stomach floor with a straw broom
Activating and beginning to love and harmonize
The parts of the light body that go out of synchronization
Through self-abuse ignorance and ignoring
The gut feelings perpetrated by outer abuse and memories
As the other brain is in our stomach
A plane is gliding silently in the sky not ominous
Like a drone can be but nevertheless unmanned
I am looking through a maze of trees from underneath
But then I realize they are my veins
And I can see them as my flesh is transparent
There is a creature like a ninja turtle
Coming towards me through a tunnel
But it is not cartoon as I can see its soft underbelly
Like a huge strange creature standing on its hind legs
Is it the hero come to rescue
The children from the underground facilities
A tree blowing almost sideways above the ground
It is dusk and I am expecting a full moon
Although it is a grey night
All that has been so active below the ground
Is only visible by the signs of strange weather
And cycles of the moon above

23. 10. 2020

A bunch of lavender
Being cultivated on the side of a road
The wheelbarrow and shovel sitting beside
The smell of sweet lavender
That fills my nostrils and calms me down
Humanity needs to calm down
And plant sweet lavender on the highways
When we calm down
We can see the bigger picture clearly
Like soldiers marching past part of a nasty game
Because they have no free will as human beings
Once we know they have been coerced and created
For the system and not for us
We can dismantle their formation
And stop the game
Take time to smell the lavender
On our way to work
And give thanks to the ones who planted the lavender
And helped it to grow on the road
So that humanity could calm down
Instead of using fake poppies
To worship dead soldiers
Who died for our freedom in fake wars
Plant lavender to calm our anxiety about this one

24. 10. 2020

Your energy my energy icons and ornaments
Symbols of intention thought and memories
Like trophies to our achievements or goals to reach
Symbols of our status that become embroiled
In our sense of self so that we do not let them go when they are no longer useful
But hoard them like trinkets already stagnant they stagnate us
But we have not let them go and so they hold us down and back
And our self-worth becomes cluttered to the point of suffocation
Learning how to let things pass is a great learning
So that new things can come in their wake
So the energy remains vibrant new and living and ever moving
Non attachment is simplicity keeping life simple in the first place
Frees us up to get on with other things without fear of attachment to things
To enjoy what this plane of existence has to offer is to live in the joy
A gift to us for our learning
That does not mean giving up simple pleasures
Of life at home and home life
Balance is the ability to know when enough is enough
Lock downs allowed us to go within freed from outer distractions
To sit with ones self is a skill to develop
Once the lock down was over we sprang back fresh and renewed
Appreciating simple things like breathing the sun rain the elements
And being in front of fellow human beings known and unknown
Eventually without masks and with new eyes with our senses more awake

25. 10. 2020

The inside of a daisy like the inside of an umbrella pattern
Beach bucket on the sand and a knotted tree stump
Turns into a fist I think it means people power
Against the beast of our own making

28. 10. 2020

A spire from the underneath
Has radiation that you can see
Spreading out from its tip
An old fashioned garden tap
People being searched at airports
And borders for anything hiding in their luggage
Draconian measures unexplained
Another antennae invented
To combat the frequency of the big tower
A personal electricity WiFi system
That generates its own power off grid
Is eating oranges a solution
For radiation poisoning
More inventions by a ghostly hand
But I can't make it out
Some sort of hose gun
And cup of tea boiling on a stove
Simple pleasures to combat
A big picture imposed on us all
One day it will all come out right
Be exposed not out of sight
Satellite dishes that take on a new role
Not used to beam up or down
Purely to keep us all under control
Sellotape in the shape of a snail
And a petrol pump for different fuel
Something looks like a fan
From the top but I think it's a motor rotor
An old fashioned electricity tower
Is shrouded in cloud

Someone is shaking
What could be a tambourine
But holding it flat side up
To collect and reflect light
All these things not yet seen in our world
For the portable unwired use
Of the everyday person
Will come to pass

30. 10. 2020

A planet floating in space is omnipresent
Radar and attempts to probe the universe
From planet earth
Tonight is a super moon so what does that mean
Why do we record phases of the moon when we are so skeptical
About other ancient sciences
Are we trying to get an insight into our own planet
By way of a window into what surrounds it
Or is this purely just another colonial exercise
Driven by testosterone and the need to conquer
Even greater domains that we do not understand in depth
And so continue to destroy the delicate balance
In which we are part of human foolishness
While we forget we are a part of the greatest divinity
And instead try to become it by diminishing it
While we keep discovering it by stuffing it all into a test tube
Can we become blinded by our own sciences
How many times do we need to go back to the beginning
And start again with a simple question
Where are we really in our physical universe

01. 11. 2020

When the flag turns to flame
But still waves in the breeze
And the moon appears from behind a cloud as full
The dawn of the age of Aquarius
Will have begun
All manner of deceptively will be laid bare
And the light at the end of the tunnel
Resembles a sick bed with nobody in it
All manner of things natural
Will be in the shadows
Until the lighthouse switches on
Inside the lighthouse looking out
The ocean stretches as far as the eye can see
And it is calm
From a perspective of greater height
We can see further and beyond
The monsters that crawl like mice
With alien eyes
Half robotic mutations
From a bygone age
The true new millennium will have begun
Once we stop being fixated
On smaller things
That make us want to jump on chairs and screech

06. 11. 2020

A facial recognition box
Comes up in the middle of a huge
White mist or cloud but it is turned sideways
The face is looking to the left
I am also thinking of the Melbourne cup
With no one at the stadium
The race
And then the horse gets put down
I remember the old Zagar and Evans song
In the year 2020 - 2025
Who needs to wait that long
When 2020 is already like this
What we need to change is obvious
To get our balance back as a human race
What is not obvious is the amount of time
It has taken to get to this point
That we have to make a quick turn around
We are needing extreme tolerance
For extreme attitudes about extreme measures
Being taken for a virus pandemic
That has been taken to an extreme
I wonder how long before the virus
Is no longer the excuse for being extreme
We need democracy in balance not high alert

07. 11. 2020

The spiral of life
The Fibonacci sequence
From which springs all things
An empty trapeze is blown in the wind
To the fronds of a fern beginning to unfold
All things held in space but not always time
Just constant movement
Now that I am more aware
Of the fifth element omnipresent
Invisible like the air but essential to life
And what birds are aware of
When they navigate the skies
What holds us in place
Wherever we move on earth and universe
Even when the other elements are not there
Earth Air Fire Water we forget space the ether
Yet without space holding the fern could not unfold
The bird could not move in the sky and find its way home
The eye of an owl or hawk is disguised by a metal hood
The ghostly memory of fire
In the trees captured like a negative photo
On celluloid imprinted in space only visible
To the few who have eyes of an owl
I started seeing machines falling over
The hood on the owls eye was industrial
The metal was steel not sure
What that was unless metal is yet
Another element of a secondary kind
Fashioned between the other elements
Of and harnessed by human intervention from

The original natural materials
They call it the alchemy
But it still obeys natural law of the space that it occupies
That delineates and fixes it in time being manufactured
Have the animals of the night become shrouded unnaturally
By human endeavor
Or is it that they have the ability to see
The fifth elements in a way that we cannot
The alchemy between elements
Then the alchemy of our engineering feats that
Defines us in a way that controls us
Is the owl wise enough to see through all that

11. 11. 2020

Ceilings and fans and a giant Indian figurine lamp
Shiva hands above the head
People walking about their business
On a street in New Delhi
Crisp white clothing
Against weather beaten old streets
A ladder in a loft at twilight
And the pitch of the roof beams
But they are not enclosed by the roof itself
A bed in the loft on the floor is unmade
The scissors and the other instruments are taken away
From the scene of an operation
As if a giant cone shape has moved them off the scene
Out of sight away from the image
Of calmness and stillness
Where they are not allowed to exist
The person in the loft
Can only rest easily and peacefully
Where fears of something nasty
Coming to get them are not visible
Blanket of stars is the remedy for a shell shocked mind
Fragmented by energies bombarding and pushing
The nervous system into fight or flight
When all the invading energies
Are removed and when the state of stillness
And peace is restored by a calm environment
That engenders a calm state of mind
Then all will be well

14. 11. 2020

With the help of female spider
I managed to keep the negative gas lighting
Away and could absorb myself
In the meaning of the decrees
Getting practice for stronger balance
I had thoughts of those who have
Been further down the rabbit hole
Of gas lighting and yet seen natural light
And now no longer wanting
To be a part of war against humanity
What horrific insight is that
What a journey back to balance
It would be I imagine impressive if Musk became
One of the ones no longer perpetrating
This nightmare for humanity planned
What a force for good could he be
To understand the lack of trust that dogs him
From human beings who wish now to rejoice
How many of us would understand that journey back
Rejoining the human race
A massive life lesson for one human being

19. 11. 2020

Message from the visitors
In my room the other night
Goes something like once
I accept I can come from the future
The extra terrestrials will start landing
Inwardly and it will make sense
When I allow myself
To be in that state of consciousness
Between waking and sleeping
As suspended animation
The letting go will be a sigh of relief
As it will allow the energy to start flooding in
Much will heal my aches and pains
And give me the strength to rise above
All the narratives going on down
Here on earth because it is a state of being
Not a state of mind
As the scary creatures with alien eyes
Are all a mythology of smoke and mirrors
Designed to keep us away
From this real state awareness
All the aches and pains
Are just a manifestation of the resistance
But this is not something
I can give to others
This can only be achieved within
To open our inner universe to the divine
Is to throw away all dogmas and preconditions
All rule books and be guided by self alone
Some others are not ready to do that

But when you think about it
The UFO phenomenon has been with us forever
Not through the eyes of the cabal
Or other manipulative societies
But always there ready for us to wake up
Through the pineal cone between the eyes
Part of the inner structure
Built into who we are
That we have been controlled through
Prevented from opening out to
Why else would they really
Lace our water with chemicals
So our internal all seeing eye
Won't work fluidity and properly

02. 11. 2020

The cockroaches got under my skin
So my friend and I were pulling them out
They mutated between a cockroach and a tick
And embed their huge bodies into our flesh
Leaving feelers exposed or bottoms up
As though they were testing the air
Half or three quarters submerged eating our insides
At the other end of the mattress we were sleeping on
There was another friend
Waving half submerged in the springs
I felt I must go and save her
I said this to the friend at my end
But I was too late I realized as I pulled her out to see
The cockroaches had already eaten her from the waist down
The evil bastards
I woke myself up this morning screaming
I will not let the cockroaches under my skin again
Cockroaches are the deep state media
That have infiltrated our bedrooms
Taken over what's left and green
Eaten us from the inside out to the point that we have to
Keep pulling them out before they get in too deep
And take away our lives
The mattress is the sleeping state
Of humanity that still believes
There are no mutations of our movements
No infiltration beneath our skin
No agenda to destroy us
We try to wake them up
But while they are half submerged in the mattress

Waving to be saved
Already half destroyed by the pestilence
Of a decayed globalist society
We learn those half eaten will not make it
That is when it is too late to save them
For this life anyway

21. 11. 2020

Libran scales for balance feeling
Where the imbalance is
Running water reverse of water boarding
Can also block out the gas lighting
And trauma when the intention is there
To rise above it and it is by choice
It is the sound that blocks
Internal conflict and chatter
Where is spider today
At the bottom of the cave
I look out at the world from
Or is it the bottom corner of my eyeball
Which are the eyes
That perceive the world from inside and out
She could be telling me there is work to do
On the base chakra where all the lower back pain is
Where it has gone out of balance
As she is such a gentle female spider
The angels put their hand
On my crown chakra to calm my anxiety
And make me aware that it is just my anxiety
Like all of us being hyped up at the moment
By world events so we can't think rationally
Which is the intention of all these hyped up events
I must calm my own body temple down
So I don't continue the battle internally
And become a sponge for all
That is not right on our planet
Becoming a mirror to other people's anxiety
Attracting anxiety and others with it as a result

The balance is to fine tune
The scales are Libran scales for that reason
It is a fine line between balance and imbalance
Like flying a plane and keeping a steady hand
To stay on the flight path
All these things will become known
In time by many people who use the tools
Thank you for the insight in this mediation today
I can balance myself better when I know what I am balancing
And to remember how to do fine tuning
When I feel hyped up
I need to take five to re balance
Go nowhere while my energy is unbalanced
In case I become scattered
And then become unsafe and ungrounded
Losing things is just a symptom
Of being overwhelmed and beginning to lose oneself
Stay strong and calm sensitive ones

02. 12. 2020

It is not hard to pick holes
In the short comings of other's friends or enemies
There will be so many it is a sieve that cannot hold water
Time to look at our own reasons
For not being able to rise above the
Negative influences of the outside and inside worlds that nag us
And keep us under control
Where is the trauma and what is the fear
Why is the voice so loud some days
While other days are easy
We are all full of idiosyncrasies
And therefore open to manipulation
Inner strength in facing your own demons
And making sure they don't contribute
To the negative energetic noise
Stay calm little one stay calm
And at peace in your own home your space
No matter how humble it is sacred to your well being
The beauty of humanity is on the rise if you know where to find it
Amid the drone of everyday enslavement
We have so willingly conceded to but that is not all the picture
Just pieces of the puzzle coming together
For now have patience all will be revealed

06. 12. 2020

An old price tag lies on the grass
Symbol of an old world cash and freedom
Of ice cream cones and fairgrounds fairies and other tiny friends
At a country market through a child's eyes
Beginnings of other lives starting to break through
The trauma zone of numbness which has been the iron curtain
Or steel door we feel trapped behind
In consciousness of ourselves and our lives and life itself
Unaware of blocking memories of other lives
Being consciously forced to open out and raise up
Above the rising dark that threatens to put out our lights
Remove our eyes and take over our souls
Too much secrecy and double dealing
In our governments to trust anyone or the vaccine
Humankind facing genocide over time but not much time
2025 is the deadline by which time
It will have turned around and we will not be alone
Left to stop it from being forced on us one way or another
Raising our antennae above the narrative
Those that are in the know and those that are not
As our governments are colluding against us all
And then the rest of the herd being herded over the cliff
All that seems to be forcing some of us into other levels of awareness
Shock awakening

08. 12. 2020

A brick on the ground
And another to better balance
Essential in this time to do nothing
Until you have a solid foundation
In yourself and your life
To stay balanced when the world
Is fragmented and out of balance
Collapsing- is beginning to show
Things are broken and we pay more
The state of flux makes us tired
People are precious to compare notes with
To congregate and discuss
A plan for renewal in difficult times
The brain can seem interfered with
Even in the absence
Of mind-altering drugs
Extreme weather catastrophic events
Are but mild symptom of a bigger disease
A paper origami boat on a real ocean
Is not a practical solution but merely an idea

09. 12. 2020

How will the governments cover up the disasters
As the numbers rise the ones affected by the vaccine
Will outnumber the ones who haven't been affected
The fear could drive more vaccine in some
While others pray over bowls
While some take the jab
There is a sense of uneasy quietness
A deathly compliance of lambs
That could still go to the slaughter
Silently like silence of the lambs
Then there will be a massive moon
Or sun arising over the earth
Like we are in a shuttle coming into land
On another planet
Like earth is being towed
And hitchhiked to a new orbit
All of this will make sense in the longer term
But the days of the darkness
Of communication breakdown
Are upon us now it seems
Out of orbit, or out of control of ourselves
While the roll out continues

11. 12. 2020

A stool with squat legs
And hands that left the stool for the spirit rising
A peacock with tail feathers down
But a feather on its head arches up
It is running like a bush fowl
Thinking about Tomomi
And Japanese ceremonies
For the dearly departed
A copper pot is like an urn
The lid comes off to send
Her beautiful soul to join the others
In the solar system
Which becomes visible once the lid is lifted
Ceremonies from another culture
Which are enriching and refreshing
As ours may or may not be to them
Death is but a cycle and a release
From this state to the next
We come from another state
Pass through this one
And rejoin the other state
On the other side
Back to the stars
A Japanese fan hides the mouth
But not the eyes
A ceremony that is completed
With a white swan
Majestic with feathers displayed behind it
Moving down a river with head bowed
Leaving us in awe of the majestic

Grace reverence and honor combined
Such is the weight
Of the state of being as we pass
And the beauty of such a sacred point
Between time as we know it
And the everlasting manifestation
Of the great creator
So soon and yet with such grace

Note:
Tomomi from our meditation group has passed away

14. 12. 2020

Sagittarius the archer shooting an arrow
Onto the roll out of the vaccine which is not all it seems
Government collusion break up the illusion
Of wealth versus poverty
Something of a blue light is shining on a scanner
Where luggage goes through at an airport
A lot of PPE and medical parade
Dramatic display for COVID 19 masks the cover up
As there are a line of people going up an escalator
Into a dome surrounded by a fluorescent blue light
Same blue light that ignites something that highlights
The vaccinated from the non vaccinated
There are no warning signs on the vile of the vaccine
And similar to taking a hit of chemo or activates like
An internal Chernobyl disaster hence the barrel says danger
I am asking what can we do to stop it being used
How will the governments cover up
The disasters as the numbers rise
Of those adversely affected by the vaccine

20. 12. 2020

Bottom end of a lunar or solar eclipse
Is visible beneath a cloud lit by the hidden sun
It is an energy shift and a re balance
Feels like coming out of madness
In mainstream creating the storm
A child on a swing in a school yard
Is enclosed by bars
Symbols of the lack of freedom
We will be leaving to the next generation
If we continue this way
Being dictated to from the outside
And caged from the inside
A vine growing is growth
From another part of my mind
Only visible in a flash
Sit quietly the change is from within
A new world is coming
Not of their making
But the elephant who never forgets
Reveals the elephant in the room
Symbols of another culture
A tyre on the runway
Only a plane journey away
But still grounded

23. 12. 2020

The rings of a tree are shown clearly when it is cut down
Simultaneous time recorded in its bark if we play a slice of wood
With a needle like an old fashioned record we get music
If this is proof that all things are already recorded
Why do we need computers in an artificial world
To collect all this data to use it against us
We have good reason to be suspicious
Why would we take away the beauty of such a beautiful and simple discovery
Artificially created science of things interfered with quantum physics
Will we be yelling at humanity to wake up more loudly
Into the Aquarian age
Or will all this settle down into a balance
If time does not exist then we can move back and forth
Through our lifetimes time travel on ourselves to change our past as we see our past
Or simply observe it to learn from it to heal our present
I see why alien races from out there are content to keep observing us
Even when there is an agenda to paint them as evil aliens
Bring up the ancient brain fight and flight response
To block them out when they have co-existed with us all this time
The ancient cultures worked with them
We have been manipulated by the few to only hear their message
Through the mouths of the few
When they are here for us all if we let them be

30. 12. 2020

A ring with stones on it promise of happier times
Where birds like magies fly sideways
Not so certain in uncertain times
Not so black and white in clear daylight
But visible enough to see
Beyond the bigger picture
Is it my wedding
Or the wedding of someone close
Traditional black and white
And the ring being put on the finger
Symbolic of a new life
What you wish for can happen
It is out there coming into the visible universe
A close up of the stone on the ring
Like an amber yellow
Not sure what precious stone
But it radiates from the centre
Good luck for a good life
In front of my face

02. 01. 2021

UFO circling raising my vibration to see it
Bird noises keep me grounded
A big day with not much to say
All is in process
Stay positive little one the bad back will go
It is just a clearing out process
And catching up on sleeping
When the rain comes
To knock us out of hyperactivity
Anxiety and depression
This cycle we are all in on the planet
We think we are alone
But we are not the only ones feeling it
A festering wound of flesh
Turns to a pile of dead leaves
In the Autumn
And Christmas will be
A real one this year

03. 01. 2021

A flower is growing within a plant time exposure
It becomes closer and brighter
But it has a stem at a right angle bent to the right
I think about it as it straightens itself up
I am staring at the veins in the stem
It is very strong just as one starts off
Growing awareness of the flower
From a distance
The flower is our awareness growing
Where we have become bent
We can straighten up
As we get stronger and closer to the truth
By that time it is no longer in the distance
But now in our reality it merges with us
And as we become part of it
We absorb its energy
And the truth of its existence

04. 01. 2021

A leap of faith
An opportunity awaits
For no matter which way
It is a new horizon
An opportunity
To spread your wings
An elephant in the room
So tired
An elephant again
Does the heavy lifting

06. 01. 2021

Arms raised above our heads
Arms bound at the wrist and joined above our heads
The difference between freedom and bondage
What binds us to remove the ropes and flow freely
As a divine being dancing in the elements
Conscious of the space we live in
What is the fifth element of space
That accommodates and records our joy and sorrow
Fill it with joy so there is no space for sorrow
Un-blindfold yourself beautiful human being
To remove self sabotage
To be more easily connected to our true self and our divine dimensions
Whatever constitutes self sabotage
Has to include the false impression we make on our friends
And what judgments our friends hold towards us in life
Seen through the shortcomings of all concerned
As we face our own to remove them
We see the shortcomings of others more easily
Eventually the habit of holding onto our shortcomings
Or our impressions of others shortcomings will diminish over time
And we can set them free into the universe
As we set them free to move onto greater things
We realize there was no obligation intended originally
Where as if we hold on to them over time we weave a web that traps us
As my spider friend says you owe nothing to anyone it is better to let them go instead

10. 01. 2021

A tube like an air-con duct
Or a mincing machine
Where the product is mixed
But the machine is not connected
A brush fire in the grass
Mickey mouse ears
Turn into giant amplifiers
A platform becomes something
You can hold in your hand
A phone is a line between dimensions
Tesla theory on quantum space
And time travel becoming visible
When we can understand how things
Can appear and disappear through a vortex
Man made or otherwise
Communication with the stars finally released
Quantum travel and time travel
Quantum leap of faith into the universe
Past the illusions of evil aliens
Perpetrated by the media
And popular culture of any time
That keeps people trapped
In their own fear
Fear of their own belly button

13. 01. 2021

The bottom of a fairground from the waist down
The legs of a draft horse a flying creature spreads its wings
Is it a dragon fly or a dragon
All manner of things
Are not as they seem
A person is riding a dragon
Not ominous but observing
The human version of a drone
So tired here on ground zero
A person in a version
Of a hazmat suit or a combat uniform
Or a uniform from a political faction
Of another country
Is turning in slow motion to look at something
They sense coming from the side or new north
The birds are cawing and cooing in the sunlight today
After so much rain
Blissfully unaware of this human drama
Being played out behind the scenes

15. 01. 2021

Moving energy from numbness
Sense of keeping balance between physical yoga
And acknowledging the light body by smudging
The importance of sound vibration and pitch
Prayer and meditation and writings
What is the cabal but base chakra split off
We all have light bodies on planet earth
Are some split from higher chakras
Stuck and embedded
We need to remove all the past and present
Traumas and blocks and being susceptible
To brainwashing and coercion as a result
The pen is mightier than the sword these days
Double edged sword of the pen
Used correctly can cut through illusions of reality
And unbalanced perceptions
Used incorrectly it can slaughter millions
Be mindful of what you write and speak
For to guide others is a privilege
So do not allow it to be abused
Remain humble in your humanness
One of humanity and admit mistakes
As you wake up to making them
Being transparent and honest will be the light
That shines through the fear
Humanity is waking up
We are the trailblazers and scrub cutters
Where the forest is so thick no one can see the trees
Follow me says the light bright on a dark highway
Humanity is in the birthing canal to a new paradigm
Where all things will be revealed
The knowledge of technology
Can still be used for good and not control
To be harnessed to balance the world

16. 01. 2021

A Chinese traditional house in the sunset on a mountain
When you take away the fear that has been whipped up
It is not so much about Chinese communism but globalism
Different cultural values and traditions
Being superimposed on other cultures
That do not recognize the original culture
Or remember how it came to be that way
It is easier to reject what you don't understand
Than stand for the truth in times of fear
This war is astral inter dimensional
Because it is conjuring many illusions
Using technology we dont understand
Some reverse engineering used negatively
While blaming a nation
That has already been subjected to that tyranny
Peoples of the earth will unite when
The common enemy is not only one race
We are all in the collective of
All that has been revealed and not revealed
Discovered and undiscovered
And what is rising to the surface to be healed
The common enemy has been described as
The tyranny of the few
And that does not depend on borders
Though it seeks to lock us all into its borders
Before we can build our own walls
To protect ourselves and reinstate our own sovereignty
What does a crab do when it has been threatened
It crawls back into its shell to hide rather than fight
Is the lock up designed to take us all back until

We find it harder to crawl out of our shell
When we do come out of being locked up
We face a barrage of everything that caused us
To withdraw into our shell in the first place
As life progresses we become conditioned to be
Frozen in time turned to stone Zombies
Locked in our own fear a self-imposed cage
Even when the cage is not there
It is time to speak up now and say NO
Even as the threat of being locked down
From the outside increases
To say NO is empowering to the soul
To cringe and hide cripples the soul over time

17. 01. 2021

Dead rose buds held up to the sky and what was a flower arrangement
With what is a dead or sleeping cat curled up at its base
A child's hand holding onto what could be a lifebuoy
The rope stand anchors the boat to the jetty but the child's hand begins to unclasp
And it is pulled away from the shore by something unseen
This right to our procreation is slipping away
A babies crib from another culture like a rocker
Ornamented by flowers but there is no child
It is a funeral preparation in Chinese culture
Such a sad state of affairs for the human race when we cut off our own survival
And no longer honor our dead such a sad exhibit to the past
Where we were once a thriving species I feel such sadness as shock and stillness
That comes with realization that the human race is already culling its own seed
Destroying our rights to celebration over birth
And giving our seed and our god given rights to be born over to an unseen force
How can we overturn what has already begun
The fact that aborted fetal tissue
Is used in our vaccines to reduce our fertility
We are beginning a mourning process for the entirety of the human race
Being deleted by our own kind of malignant technology

20. 01. 2021

An old armchair
A fist held up with thumb protected
Lights like orbs around the fist
Signs of humanity standing up
Protected and guided by spirit
What could be a compass turns into a shower rose
And then a screw unwound
Waiting for where it has to go in preparation
The shower rose now turns into a rose
Whose petals have fallen
How much time do we have to prepare for an event
That has come and gone
Behind closed doors silently
A giant screw going into the earth
Drilling for something or laying a foundation
Or saying we are all screwed
There are big things afoot for us all
Bread sticks in a camp chair
The bread sticks are real
But the camp chair is not manifest
Food preparation for many
Dimensions not yet quite visible
To the naked eye

24. 01. 2021

Green leaves sprout sideways Santorini
Italian meal celebration
Vatican oppression is gone
And life has lightened
Bounced back into new life and freedom
Blotches of rain on the camera lenses
From where I am filming
A single person on a park bench looking at water
But it is just a still life
The water is not running
Breaking through the illusion of mask wearing
That look like bird beaks
With no breathing apparatus
A still life version of reality is paper thin
About to break out of the text book
Of rules and regulations
They tried to reign in our reality
In between new growth of real foliage
We get a glimpse of a new world beyond
The invisible cage we have been in for centuries

28. 01. 2021

Spinning wheel of lazar light
Multi wheel is an energetic re calibrating
Demagnetizing tool held over the body it rotates and realigns
Hand held behind a smudge stick pushes it towards me
It becomes a papyrus scroll as it comes closer
The walls behind it huge and ancient become visible
Something fits into pharaohs times
As the stones sit into each other each stone is taller
Than a human and weighing tons
They are saying read the hieroglyphs it is time
A messenger carries a scroll in real moving time describing an event
That is then recorded in the hieroglyphs speaking of an astrological alignment
In the future now to be unraveled
What was known to the ancients cannot be destroyed by human hand
Even if the artefacts have been removed as visible markers to ancient knowing
The archives is recorded in our chakras our light body akashic records
It is sad to lose the physical touchstones of the ancient ones from our visible universe
By those who want to hide the truth from coming out
But it is just a slight of hand because the truth will come out anyway
The narrative of human history will change also accordingly
And the ancient artefacts can be reconstructed
From 3D printing machines and memory of atomic structure

29. 01. 2021

A fist opens in front of a cave entrance
And reveals an old sage at a writing desk
Who looks up when he sees the light at the entrance
All will be revealed from a dark cave
When the light is shed upon it
The entrance is opened by a determined hand
That holds the truth tightly and yet lets go lightly
There is a celebration surrounding a wreath of flowers
A ceremony from ancient times
In the distance an explosion lights up the sky
Another jigsaw puzzle piece but three dimensional
A hand is putting on a glove or is it being peeled off
Something skims under the water at the speed of light
While an old fashioned washer woman in uniform
Stands behind a steel rimmed wooden washing bucket
Time has collapsed as we know it
Says the man from the cave who was predicting future times
Quantum physics and the birth of the Age of Aquarius
Were always designed to bring us
Into a new paradigm of human consciousness
Weeding out the dark all cloaked in secrets

Research: This came the same day as Biden signed the executive order to put the environment first regardless of current human needs and enterprise

06. 02. 2021

The feather that you identify with or
The quill that you write your story with
Upon the chambers of your heart
Is your birthright
And the acknowledgment of your birthright
As well as the journey there on in
From your childhood onwards
There is no one and nothing
That can make you sign that away
Even though the birth certificate
Entered you into a contract
With a marine corporation
In recent years
Over the last few hundred years
They do not and cannot
Own your soul
Or take control of what is divine
Your human rights will be reinstated
The day you stand up and take them back
As the roulette wheel for money is moved aside
Rumpelstiltskin will be named as the perpetrator
And the contract will be made null and void

10. 02.2021

Angel fish orange and white stripe clown fish
Messenger of the ocean as above
So below a beacon to the reef
Home of the newborn cradle of birth
Practice with good will
What will bring harmony and balance
To the delicate balance that is life
Restore the balance
Regrowth of the life of the reef
In a tank
Beginning with the awareness
And then the knowledge
From there we can swim
To the surface of the tank
That lets the light in resurfacing into
A very bright world and returning
To the original home where we belong

Research: the great barrier reef being destroyed in its natural habitat is being recreated in a tank

16. 02. 2021

What could be posies of flowers turns into something more ominous
But yet unseen as to what it is so I am aware that I am spun out
And need to stay grounded by finding a routine of meditation and relaxation
It is not over yet as it has only just begun rings in my ears
I am alone in the mountains with La Nina rain outside again
My lawns grow too quickly so what will this season bring
Stay in the present not knowing the future forces us to stay in the present
No one can plan when we do not know
The birds outside in the rain and the smell of a sage stick just burned
Are my only comforts as well as a beautiful little cottage
That is sometimes hard to appreciate without company
Learning to sit with myself and my own truth

Research: Mercury appearing as the morning star

26. 02. 2021

A stick is planted above the ground
In a huge tilled open field
It is twilight
Was it the moon the sun
A planet or a UFO
Flying away from the site
Symbol of hope
Above the ground will begin again
The twig or olive leaf plant
Has been planted
Many images pass by
Overlapping in my mind
Each has a story or thread
Of what has just happened
And is still playing out
But it is overlapping
Many will be damaged
By the illusions
Perpetrated on the masses
But now the truth
Has been planted
Above the ground
It only has to grow and prosper
One day the field will be green again

27. 02. 2021

The baby that you missed so sadly
Still occupying a space in that cavity
Needs to be acknowledged
Your body remembers or still holds the memory
The witches hat is also a spire and a pyramid
The geometric shape has significance
Not as an obelisk but the female equivalent
Used throughout eons
As sacred geometry in ancient times
The body remembers interference from eons ago
As a female throughout history
The misinformation perpetrated upon us still exists
The underneath of a bowl that feeds us
Behind which are witches with crooked noses and warts
Around a pot of another kind made out to be the perpetrators
Dammed by the slammers such an ugly image
To prevent the divine feminine from shining throughout
Or rising out of the distorted darkness of the underworlds
I smell rose petals In my meditation room
The divine feminine is rising within me not broken but ever present
In spite of how we only recorded human HIStory

28. 02. 2021

A flower comes out of a top hat
It is a rose but is it a real flower or a trick
The mists of illusion are still around
The image half submerged but it is emerging
As the mists recede it becomes clearer
Propellers of war fuselages but there is no plane
We are being shown half truths so that we will slip
Back into illusion by imagining the rest with our conditioned minds
Meanwhile the real story slips back into the mists of time
It is important to wait because the rest of the truth
Is not as we imagine it
Like the magicians trick will you see that dark pink rose in reality
Or the red plastic flower when the magician has finished
The magic illusion means
Many things will come out of the top hat
But we must be patient until the trick is over
Once our illusions are shattered
And we can understand the mechanism
Behind The Greatest Show On Earth
As presented by The Ringmaster
Introducing the acts or presenting the images
He is pulling more and more
Out of the hat to play with our perceptions
But we can choose to focus on the flower
As the pink rose is also the lotus in the heart

02. 03. 2021

A posy of flowers or a bunch of violets
Comes out held by a skinny arm
Coming from behind an altar font and a curtain
There are blessings and good news to be had
There are things to be revealed in public domain
That were forbidden and hidden behind the church baptism font
There will be a sigh of relief and a breathing in once more
The posy has turned into a mix of flowers
Like a child would gather from the side of the road
The perpetrators are being made known
Now the children are not to be silenced
They are coming out from behind the altars
Even though their faces are not visible
We see their arm of truth and they are offering a gift of the truth
To all the congregations of all of humanity
Who will finally be able to look at what is in plain sight
The children still have beauty in that they want the truth to be seen
They hold another banner to the world and the cross on their tombstones
Can no longer be seen as a curse or worshiped in ignorance
Of what it became or what has been done in the name of the fathers
The sins of the fathers are being exposed by the children they abused

06. 03. 2021

A letterbox on a barren highway without a house in sight
Dirt fields surrounding could be furloughed or maybe they are just dry
Ned Kelly armor has fallen on the ground beside the mail box
Like the infamous legend about the outcast from society
The Robin Hood of Australia is no longer in battle mode but there is no one here either
The letterbox symbol of communication remains like a beacon
To what was once our only way of connecting as human beings in the outback
The battle is over but in its wake the houses and people are silent and disconnected
A single piece of paper or is it a chip packet blows like artificial grass along the outback highway
A sign that life was once there but how long ago as we have no need for Ned Kelly now
Was he really who they said he was a warrior for the underdog on the outback highways
A symbol of uprising against a corrupt government
Where outlawed people took their power back
By donning home made armor to fight a visible war
In front of the mass of humanity was Ned Kelly
The infamous criminal put on a pedestal
By an oppressed people at a difficult point in Australian history
Whatever way we look at it his armor is lying on the ground now
The story has been twisted like a metal arm barely recognizable
But somehow a powerful reminder of past uprisings
Where we have needed someone to lead us out of desolation
To remind us we are the fighters who survived a barren landscape
In isolation to tell the tale back then and now that the mailbox is also obsolete
Where are the tinpot warriors of a wasteland that has become an outback trashcan now

07. 03. 2021

A tablet from ancient times in a crypt and alcove of a wall
Written in ancient Hebrew or hieroglyphics begins to burn
A man walks a street in Israel purple flowers climbing a wall at his side
A church spire with a cross and a scribes hand in a glove or is it automated
Where canceling our culture plans to rob us of our history no matter how distorted
And wipe our lineages clean like an unwritten slate ready for artificial"everything"
Leaving us soulless in more ways than one until what we value in life
Will no longer make sense without the threads to connecting what was once
A rich and resplendent cultural evolution over millennia
With its scribes writing on ancient tablets
Now burning with a strange flame that has not burned all the evidence
But one side of the encryption that is no longer
Maybe in future times with the right equipment we will be able to replace
What was destroyed in real time
Meanwhile people are unaware that they are contributing to their own demise
Canceling themselves in context rendering themselves soulless for a counterculture
That seeks political correctness at all costs as it removes the evidence of how we got here
Soon there will be a rebellion against the rebellion of another counterculture
We can only hope it is put back the way it originally was
And not rejigged to suit yet another agenda to control us all

10. 03. 2021

A heart being grown artificially turns into a jellyfish under the water
Reeds tied together turn into multiple arrows shooting towards a target
The corner of an eye turns into a goat with horns facing backwards
Genetically modified chromosomes colors of the rainbow turning white
On a spinning top as humankind is on a roulette wheel
Spinning the wheel to see where we land and what we have got is not a safe solution
Finger and a thumb holding a tiny insect
Is it real or created by Artificial Intelligence or a bot
We are opening our hands to a blank screen to create anything like a hologram
But will the pioneers of science pay a huge price for modifying the genes of all things
Looking backwards through the pages of an old encyclopedia with pictures
In a huge old library that smells of mothballs like Harry Potter where the pictures jump out into life
What reference will we have when our world is reduced to a flat piece of fabric like plastic
Held between a thumb and forefinger from which springs
The matter of all that matters to us then

Research J.K. Rowling and Dr Seuss are under the hammer

12. 03. 2021

Energy Brother Aliens Egypt
Thoughts of why not Nephilim giants why else are we so minute
Compared to Egyptian architecture
A red rosebud beginning something as a rose blooms in a desert
A purple rose instead of a rock striking out on another level
Opening out to new dimensions
More connected to the stomach chakra
Great to feel more centered and grounded
In early days of remembering how it felt
To have that part of the body and chakra working
We dont realize we are not working on all cylinders
Until the one that wasn't working crank starts again
Difference between feeling half awake and alive or half asleep and dead
We have all been punched in the stomach by this pandemic
The Ides of March more rain out west
Awakening in the body regeneration of spirit
New activities beginning to bud from what was planted

Research New full moon in Aquarius

13. 03. 2021

Horse hoof getting re shod been doing the miles
We can walk five hundred miles oh we can walk
The rooftop of a horse stable
The moon is full and has come out from behind the clouds
With a perfect outer ring like a halo
There are birds singing in the sunlight the next day
As we wonder where we have been
It's a journey inward and a long one already for the human race
But we must walk our talk with determination
Somehow horses are like the leaders
Who carry the burden of our trail blazing
But they have to be re shod when the shoes have worn down
Taking time out to realize this is what it is and not to be discouraged
Use it as a recharge to keep going knowing you know the way forwards

14. 03. 2021

An image icon of a house like a loan finance logo that becomes real
At least the chimney is three dimensional and the rest is clearing
The scent of someone beautiful new and yet familiar
Time of unexpected events and new meetings a newcomer in ones life
The kids in the playground outside are screaming over a footie match
Intermittently between the screech of a black bird probably a magpie
It's not so bad here summer is cooling down soon the wood of the fire
Will add its flavor to the days and nights filled with stars
That will be a beautiful transition between seasons
Being thankful for what you have
It is worth billions of stars to be grateful
And that will see you through

15. 03. 2021

A giant pill sitting on the spike of a mountain becomes the magic pill
People are praying for the pill sitting at the tip of hands in prayer
But what are we praying for a magic bullet
Now the pill turns into a bullet big and brassy like the agenda behind it
Not designed to help us antiquated technology against a bio weapon
Wrong weapon for a war on a tiny virus
Fed by misinformation and government agendas to get us to comply
To yet another thing that will take us under
An old fashioned flash camera from early world war two
Tells the story of a time when all these false narratives
Were first infiltrated into public as propaganda
When the camera lenses were first designed to capture us in their image
The earliest surveillance went underground into our sewers
Only to come back up through our vents into our streets
Like a giant mutated cockroach plague that we have to eradicate without adequate tools
It is hard for us all to believe our systems could have turned against us that much
But I would rather wake up now than be half eaten by a cockroach

23. 03. 2021

A broken piece of the jigsaw puzzle has an elephant on it
The elephant becomes real in the wildlife
Trumpeting at the joy of its own freedom
Playing in the mud and puddles beneath its feet
It is flooding in real time all over New South Wales
It could be seen as divine intervention regarding the vaccine roll out
Maybe being pulled into another emergency will force our government hand
Who will delay their plans briefly as fewer people will want to take the jab
After more adverse reactions are recorded people
Are waking up but they needed more time
Nothing like a bit of rain time to reflect
On this artificial gene being injected into our bodies
It remains to be seen what the government will do with all the additional information
And what the people will do with it once they are more awareness
Of the complicit game the government plays with big pharmaceutical corporations
Who plan to have too much money
The missing piece of the jigsaw puzzle is an elephant who never forgets
Which is also the elephant who is not in the room and symbolic
Of the trumpeter who is missing from office while the political mayhem
Plays out in the USA and while we were waiting for a new savior
We had to turn to save ourselves as a human race
And the rains brought temporary intervention
To the plan to roll out the end game in our local area

24. 03. 2021

A false flower Anzac poppy made of wire
Clasping a gem at its centre a measure of past events created
False flags and abuse of the human spirit where trauma has been registered
In the soul memory of the DNA all these things that caused us to sabotage ourselves
And not realize who our friends really were before the government tried to divide us
Those friends who could could have been closer than we are to ourselves
But for fear of facing the trauma we rejected the friend and ourselves
Which accentuated our pain
The heart grieves the loss of closeness that a true friend gives
Like a home we cannot enter until we have removed the cause of our separation
And recognize what fear holds us all backwards from taking that step
Nearer to the ones that could help us
There is trepidation in case the friend becomes a wounded dog that attacks
We hesitate where the cold outside the heart is familiar
We do not trust enough to step inside yet not to step inside hurts also

31. 03. 2021

The rainbow is like a jagged flame of a gas fire gas lit
So many variations of the true source of humanity
God and what it is to be a human being
The gas flame is not a true rainbow even though it can show the light spectrum
Those rainbows are the mirage within the flame that could be luciferian
Gas lit by the mirrors and mirages of the snippets of information
Passed down to a humanity who cries out to be released from being gas lit
Meanwhile the true rainbow is above our heads and inside our being
All things in third dimension composed of split light
All is a reflection unto this state if being no one thing is the only reflection
As we come further out into the light of day rather than the light of gas
We will realize what is gaslight and what is daylight
At the moment humanity is still going through the dark night of soullessness
The dark before the true dawn of the Age of Aquarius

01. 04. 2021

Children embrace each other as innocent babies
They share their love with extended family
There is no reason to be afraid
Their love is powerful and it penetrates
We have to remember love without fear even though
We are heavily traumatized
As long as we can remember the innocence of love
We can return there and we can create many things
But without the innocence of love there is no meaning
It is what drives us to stay alive
So how to become unstrapped from behind the window pane
That looks out at the wild weather over a stormy ocean
How to find the balance between protection and slavery
That we have to negotiate every minute of our lives as they progress
We only lose that balance when we lose our inner child
If one child can embrace another child
Even though the other child is polar opposite
Then they become welcome in the family circle
The other child only has to accept the invitation to enjoy
Love innocence and freedom to become bonded

06. 04.2021

A V shape V for vaccine heavily loaded letter of the alphabet
Sometimes we have to take a break and rise above the narrative war
That brings about our inertia
Taking a break is sometimes all it takes to turn a V
Back into a peace sign or reverse the f..k you
We are up against all things in polarity in order to find a way
To make peace with ourselves and the human race
Kitchen sink they say everything but the kitchen sink
The sink is clean before and after the garbage is washed away
A cat licks up the split milk and a frog exposes its belly
Nature is complicated but it finds a way
A clean sink can look clean when it is not
As all evidence of the interference is wiped away
We must stand up and bring our fellowman to accountability

08. 04. 2021

Green foliage leaf evergreen
Jesus and the Ascended Masters in candle white glowing white and expanding
Michael and the Angelic Realm
Lights dual street lamps divine assistance
The spinning top is moving fast as the colors of the rainbow turn to white
There is an energy and vibration that is visible and creates a wave
Of expanding dimensions from the centre
All manner of things are on the move now even as we hold our hands in prayer
There is an electrical energy field emanating from that intention
Pray for it will manifest in your dreams so seize the day and be humble
Yet mindful of what is to come for all good things come
To those who wait and have waited the time is near
The coast is clear and all will be revealed within a hairsbreadth of the activity
The monster that had us in a cave looking up at a bright blue patch of sky
Is gone and we are free to climb out of our dungeons to meet the bright new day
The old media has gone away and the new media is on its way
Celebrate in your own way

Research: The boat stuck in the Suez occurred shortly after this writing

18. 04. 2021

A mist comes in to envelop a small herbal lavender plant
Like a giant hand recognizing and reaching down
To even the most humble conscious living thing
A spinning umbrella from underneath
Where only the framework is left
A hovering craft with a humming noise
Opens a portal to spotlight the ground near the plant
Like an automated eye looking at a simple plant
With the power to relieve anxiety one of natures master pieces
More craft saucers this time at a greater height but below cloud
Scanning the landscape
It has been a long time since I wrote
Earth has already moved into the new paradigm
Even though our media refuse to admit it
The craft are now visible to the naked eye
It is confronting for humanity sign of our interference
That we cannot become so simple and so we need the wisdom
Of that plant to relieve our anxiety to regain the wisdom
We have become blindfolded from the power of sage lavender and other herbs
Until they became our smudge stick again for that very reason

29. 04. 2021

When the hand holds a crystal ball but it is black
Or the hand that cups the moon has gone dark
It is not easy to go into the future
And see the brightness of a new world coming
Until the fairy lights come on inside the ball
To show a celebration at night that will mark the beginning of
Something new and exciting out of something old and decayed
Be aware of your thoughts before the real celebration
Of a new future coming that will turn the crystal ball to white
There will be a few false starts or smaller events designed
To confuse humanity into believing this is it when it is not
Beware the false prophets with large egos even if they have
Well intentioned hearts

12. 05. 2021

As time as we know it is moving as events unfold
As the media remains a permanent block to the truth of what is changing
Humanity is again forced by an unseen hand to turn inwards
To search the far reaches of the soul to unbind from those systems
And beliefs and people that have controlled us
As we move forwards the unseen hand becomes visible
And palm up carries us across deep waters
And above the landscape in the palm
Of a giant hand that is not malevolent
But a kindly giant which can cradle many and then set us all down
On dry land somewhere that we can grow and prosper
In the truth of what it is to be a human being

21. 05. 2021

When you feel an imbalance within yourself use these tools to send
Concentrated beams of the rainbow spectrum
Into those parts that need structural re alignment
Become aware of all of your senses and which one is dominant
Bring the others up to the same frequency
If it is smell add light and seeing
If it is sound add smell and taste and touch
Eventually all the senses will begin to reactivate..at once
And your life will once again return to vibrance
And so the vibration is raised like a propeller it lifts you up
And out of dark and restricted places to embrace the present
By being present realigned with all your senses
Including space and present time which is all encompassing
So no past or future thoughts need interfere
This is how wildlife survives and maintains
Perfect power of balance within itself
So realign with it as well

23. 05. 2021

Sometimes recognizing our humanity
Feels like a tree in a desert
With a long trunk that stretches out of sight
Before the foliage begins
To spread out like a canopy umbrella
To shelter all
That live in its shade
Just as we too have to get beyond our limitations
And stretch up into the blue sky while our feet
Remain firmly planted in the earth.
Just as we sometimes feel the effort of getting there
Before we can finally
Spread out and celebrate
On an endless journey
There are so many scars and battle wounds
We can lose sight of where we were destined to go
Before we realize who we really are

26. 05. 2021

A blue corona in the sky a part of the galaxy
Now visible to the naked eye blends into the sun
Or does the sun come before and reflect illumination on the core
Things in the universe are on the move
Plants and animals know there is a recharge
Like my friends battery that just went flat
And then got restored once more
Time to contemplate the universe
And consciousness of the big One
For all is before you now the door
Is open wide to explore the universe
Of multiple dimensions
Rather than by perceptions and guesswork

Research: Night of the super blood moon solar eclipse in Sagittarius

27. 05. 2021

A sword is in its scabbard and it is ready
The very sweet smell of Daphne flower
A person in spirit is skipping freely in joy
Behind a blue shield that was once a mask
That they have taken off
It is time to follow the lead of the ghosts and spirits
Against those behind the mainstream media
That impose restrictions that will not stick
Humanity is aligning with the angels now
Not behind the facade of the
New Normal but the Realigned
There is a ring with stones on it
A giant ring and people are its gems
Standing on a platform getting the message out
Binding humanity into a marriage
Of the truth that cannot be told openly
They are the gems and the truth speakers
Who will bind our future commitment
These people are uniting now
And the sword is ready to slay
The perpetrators of false intentions
There is a crack in the cage that imprisons us
And the light is streaming in
So soon the cage will break open for a new humanity

01. 06. 2021

Eating porridge in the morning
Rooftops of traditional Chinese houses
Many narratives woven in between the tipping point for humanity
Many people many points of view narratives stolen and distorted
Half and three quarter truths in the wake of the super full blood moon
Eclipse in Sagittarius Rise Humanity Rise
For the new solar eclipse in gemini will see many more like you and me
No longer clinging to old world narratives of a conditioned past
Pavlov's dog theory only works on the greedy
When you know what you are trading for crumbs you will not so easily cave in
Why would you choose the jab lured by an ice cream or doughnut
Only to be staring out of a cage or in a coffin in five years time

Post lunar eclipse

Research: Minors lured by doughnuts and ice creams to take the jab

13. 06. 2021

Many images during prayer
Thoughts from research I have done
I have chosen the witch emerging
From the spire of a church steeple
That could also be the spike of her hat
There is a light around the church spire
That moves to her belly
And I can see she is the weather vane
She is perched up there to
Check which way the wind is blowing
I think she is like me she is the symbol of
Demonized divine feminine
And as it is a long break between writings
I am aware that I have been consumed with collating
And typing up a whole year of writings
It has been a massive journey for us all
Through out the lock down of despair
The light has moved to her midriff
Which is about the centre of the broom
There is some healing to go on
There regarding fear but never fear
Being perched up on the church steeple is a privilege

19. 06. 2021

A perfectly circular rainbow and a bird swooping within it that turns into a plane
The beauty of flight smooth and spacious and pure joy for a bird
A toilet in a garden not enclosed saying out of every bucket of shit
And another plant that looks like a stock which could be the stock market
Out of our hard ship and hard times we grow a garden on many levels
To feed many ecosystems even the tiny insect with transparent wings
Can identify with the whole thing
But dont get stuck on flying ants or gnats because it is microscopically fascinating
Instead prepare yourself for the big things and then they will come
Just as they were planned eons ago but there is more
A blackbird hovers on a wrought iron fence
Looking at what was once a patio to an elite family
It is a guilded cage but it is empty now all that remains of a story now unseen
But for a tiny flame on a candle that was once a candelabra
On a rusty chain a half remembered dark ceremony done at night
While a woman crouched forward on a huge high backed chair for a priestess
Is holding her stomach in pain wearing white but remembering dark things done at night
She is out now and safe but for the memories masked as stomach pain

21. 06. 2021

A monkey wrench a lightning rod
What is it going to take humanity
To lift us off our foundation and wake us up
Beyond our current situation
The opera house and a metronome
Ticking sideways
Say there is a fox in the hen house
A maiden with long flowing hair
Is sent to seduce and convince us
How can we be soothed
Or frightened into action
A mountain and a waterfall
Can overcome us with awe at this planet we inhabit
Or will it be a diary we are compelled
To write in out of immense loneliness
While the world is shut down around us
And we are feeling locked out

24. 06. 2021

The nose of a wild cat or a marsupial
And all manner of plants
Grown upside down in pots
Hanging from the roof
Like a light bulb in some cases
They are still growing but sideways
A garden in a greenhouse
Is beautiful and grows
The right way up
There is a wooden crutch
Leaning against a plant
Symbolic of dependency
On the greenhouse
That is the new crutch for a new life
A light is coming towards me
In front of me and gaining ground
Is it a plane or a craft
In the dark moving closer
And getting bigger than me
The beams spread out
And I hope it doesn't get so blinding
I feel run over with what is coming

02. 07. 2021

Always seeing UAP or UFO in meditation
Ships in the sky...why
Over the fields near my new block what is their purpose
We havent got part of the disclosure
Or disclosure only in part
The rest of the truth is within my own heart
It's not that I'm looking on a daily basis
But they want to turn up in my meditations it seems
Maybe to intervene in what would be otherwise
A loss of human hopes and dreams
They seem to be here and very close
But never too open to the naked eye
Unless they are man made holograms
Objects deliberately placed in strategic places in the sky
To trick and direct human consciousness
With another reverse engineered false flag
In the near future could feel overwhelming
And moving very fast in simultaneous time
It has become hitched by a wire to my garden stake
In the greenhouse
The day things come at us that fast
We need to rise up and say hey not hi or hello
A posy of cut flowers but it is the last one
In a bucket of water all the rest are gone
So is this a last opportunity for one more happy event
Before all the opportunities
To rescue ourselves are all taken
The marsupial is a wild rodent
Of some kind and it is sniffing me out
There is a house with a pitched roof that reminds me

Of a building loan logo it feels like Switzerland
And something about our currency will it float above
The disasters predicted and how
Will the housing market
Re hook itself to another franchise if that is the word

04. 07. 2021

When the mind is chattering like a squirrel
And the wheels of the world are about to fall off
Except the wheel looks a bit like a plastic one
From a child's billy cart
I am reminded it's time to respect myself
After a season of eclipses
And Saturn square Uranus in 2021
Unexpected events up against the system
Lets hope not of the pre planned variety behind closed doors
There is an extractor fan in an enclosed room
Growing or manufacturing crystals
Beautiful emotions pass me by but I cannot catch them
They are fleeting so I just have to go with the flow
There is a magnetic grid that controls the ebb and flow
Of all of our human emotions that one is natural and cyclic
Why would we want to replace that one
With the man made variety that controls our population
And pull ourselves out of alignment with the universe

09. 07. 2021

Was the Archangel Michael a spaceman from another galaxy
And all the Elohim of divine light in first there was the light spectrum
A filament under a microscope is moving an arrow pointing it away from being the focus
Of attention for human genetic wars synthetic fibres half robotic and half biological
Part of the warfare inter cellular it is time to blow up our illusions
And bomb the artefacts of world war three with an old battery on a dirt road
And with a stick of dynamite the arrow has turned to a bow and arrow
Knights and days of old 1066 Normans and Saxons back to the Magna Carta
Where new things can emerge hidden inside the rubble
Of a bombed system and an ancient ruin

11. 07. 2021

As we come into August 2021
The daffodils will begin to bloom
All manner of flowers like small hopes
Not posies but the beginnings
Of a new hope of a real spring
Individual flowers among the disinformation
That is being chipped away at
Like a pick axe hiding in the daffodils
Gradually removing the false agenda
The false hope of relief
From pandemics will end
With a real end and a new beginning globally
A table outside with a cloth
Is preparing for a feast
The truth is springing back
To life after the winter of our discontent
There is a disclosure of a new kind
As a spaceship comes into view in real time
Hovering so low over the landscape
It is time to stop the cover up of the inevitable
The technology to reverse the evil effects
Of what was in the wrong hands is here
And is about to be revealed in real time
Time to count our blessings and pick wild flowers from fields

13. 07. 2021

An energy from Egypt and a house from Mongolia
Rooftops silhouette against a huge sun
What could be a door knocker in the shape of a person
Is bending down to sift something looks like gold panning
An empty bed has been made for a while surrounded by
A canopy of flowers to someone who has passed on
A rolled up mat is symbolic of an ending
A cow is mooing in the receding mist in real time
There is a newborn baby in a crib with a hood
And an empty lolly jar on a shelf I am unscrewing the jar lid
And putting something into it
It has been left barren
For some time like fallow fields
That will someday soon spring back to life
In a new beginning a new life there is a busy street
From the past in Mongolia post this latest global lock down

25. 07. 2021

There is an image but someone has ripped out a piece of it
So now it's hard to know if it was a house
The paper looks like tinfoil or blue side building paper
Imagery is not very clear when it's not all there
Because it keeps changing going up in smoke
Crumpled up paper in a large hand
In an office making decisions over land and country
But where is everybody
The office feels empty and pointless
It is there in name and position only
In a skyscraper with a view of city rooftops
At least eight floors down there is an ocean too
But all is empty devoid of human input
Symbolic of the soulless corporate greed once thriving
But the people have left a long time ago and their energy too
I think they probably headed for the hills
Even my pen wont work recording this non event
I hear the waves crashing on our past human mistakes
Like the wind in the trees on this mountain

28. 07. 2021

Where there is a spotlight on the ground on a dark night
But the only thing in the spotlight is mickey mouse
Then we know humanity is in the dark
The corner of a plane showing me many propellers
Moving and maneuvering at a massive speed
Tells me it is wartime
But the sound outside my meditation room
In the morning is calm and comforting
Like the chorus of birds
A few realities being played out take refuge in the daylight
But be aware of what is under the spotlight
A single wild flower is growing in my minds eye
Time for the individual to grow outside of the group
The plant can become everlasting when it is dried
Which tells me individual growth is everlasting
Be concerned only
With those who come into your line of vision
Whether it be in your sleep or in the daylight
For those are the ones who are ready
There are other kinds of wild flowers
Beginning to show their heads now
I cannot identify the variety but they are well known
For their everlasting qualities

11. 08. 2021

I did not want to start recording the images immediately
So much depth of emotion
On many levels after a break in writings
And so much has happened in Australia
With our draconian government lock downs
Now I feel like I am in world war three
Or world war two revisited and continued
I can almost see the perpetrators
Change the modern-day clothing
For nazi uniforms and there you have it
Feeling for humanity and all its various stages
Of waking and sleeping dragging us further into the net
By ramping up the cases scenarios and false positives
Now I see the tree with dead leaves at sunset in winter
The leaves could be bats if I use my imagination
But I am being told the dead leaves have to fall
Sunrise brings a new winter day where the tree is laid bare
For all to see but it IS sunrise
Meanwhile broccoli is not a bad thing to eat
When you are in shock the kind of shock that wakes you
Not the one that puts you to sleep now I feel for the children
Who are now adults speaking for the children who have
Climbed out of cult satanic abuse such a huge risk
To speak about the unspeakable crimes we must now defeat

16. 08. 2021

A dark horse with a lighter mane is cantering towards me
The mane is flying in the air like flames
There is a message that is not so dark anymore
There is a tool to fix it and a survival kit for emergencies
A torch is magnetically attached to the side of a portable fridge
Ready to shine the light on the truth when that time arrives
The horse has stopped now to deliver the message
About crates of what could be alcohol
Whisky that is an old fashioned medicine
Delivered by horse and cart
You can turn a horse into a dragon
If you fear it but it may only be a rooster
Ready to crow in the dawn for us all to hear
Only I notice the rooster has its eyes closed
It may be the message is not being heard outwardly yet
Meanwhile inside the roosters eye
The sun streams over the side
Of an oriental style boat sunrise or sunset
An indigenous conche shell player
Calls the forces and heralds the elements
For the new day is about to emerge
The forces of nature will rise
From their ancient invisible portals to join us
When it is time

20. 08. 2021

There is an insect on a photocopy machine
It is bloated like it has been distorted
It is the full size of the plate
But the midriff is blown up uncomfortable
A bit like all forms of media fake or real at the moment
Blowing up sections of this or that
For effect or counter effect in fact they become an insect
Like a cockroach when the truth is not proportionate
It happens when everyone is running
To keep the momentum of the story
And keep the agenda alive
To feed humanity when really
It has all become a cockroach
Feeding off humanity that is why the cockroach
Fills the photocopy machine
So how does the truth get out there
In a world full of propaganda
And bursting with counter propaganda
Trying to move the focus
All designed to railroad us in a direction
I hear "sit still little one and go within
For therein lies your answer"
We need to stop cleaning our teeth with a nail file

21. 08. 2021

Images remind me of 9/11 Twin Towers
But they are just reminders of a past era
A boat steering wheel makes me think of my birth certificate
And being sold on the stock market
We are not sure whether to go north south east or west
Turning madly this way and that
Many things go on behind the scenes
Something is being bolted down with steel
There is an old fashioned ornate street lamp
And blank paper at the top of an old fashioned typewriter
Someone is typing also in feather and quill from earlier times
Simultaneous writing is this the new day
Before the new day is announced
A massive fan for a fanfare is being prepared
Time to wake up the masses from their sleep
A helicopter is landing I see the blades
It is daylight on an orange sort of day
The last of the components are coming together
To prepare the day time to detox from our old ways
D.T. is walking down the ramp from the helicopter
Not a grand entrance but yet planned entrance
To welcome the new day
A wounded heart takes time to heal
Like the trees take time to grow

31. 08. 2021

As we move closer to the darkness
The light becomes more obvious
As we grow closer to the light
The dark becomes more obvious
Regardless of the stories tales and agendas
Beyond the obvious
We can see for the first time into the oblivious
What was hidden in the caves concealed from us
From and throughout antiquity
Blessed be me and three geometry
A flying insect spreads out its wings
But it is frozen in time
The photocopier is pushed aside
By a cartoon character
Cross between sponge bob
And a version of Ned Kelly
A silhouette is but a shadow of no substance
We have become addicted to our own inventions
From our own narratives copied thousands of times
Until the very cartoon characters we invented
Have to stop the copying

04. 09. 2021

The flame has been lit and the chair is revolving
As we come into alignment with ourselves
And our greater purpose in the universe
All that will be revealed as we spin
We think we are spinning out
But it is just that the chair is spinning
We are moving around the 360 degree question
Of why we are here and what is our purpose
What is humanity and
Why has humanity descended to this point
How are we going to rise up
As we sit in our own hot seat
The focus is on us
To see the answer to that question
In 360 degrees from where we sit

15. 09. 2021

It feels like I am needing a re-calibration of myself
Like I am on an operating table
Made of see through glass
Staring at a huge lamp above my head
All the ghosts from another world
Are all staring down at me
Like ghost busters in reverse
Or warthog aliens
Then I turn into a jellyfish
Or is it that they turn into something else
Plasma is a bit jellyfish like
Needing to come out into a new day
And it is a beautiful day today
Want to hear the birds sing
And not see them turn their rear ends
On me to poop in my eye
It is time to take a deep breath little one
The forces of change are upon us all
Soon the way will be clear
And the road ahead unfettered uncluttered
And open to all but the compromised
The jellyfish shoots through the water
Like an octopus at lightning speed
Happy to be back in its natural environment empowered

18. 09. 2021

When the fly is a giant bug with multiple eyes
Right up against your face
When you hold your hands
In prayer but your wrists are handcuffed
And your hands wither with arthritis
While time is speeding up
To the point where that process
Is visible in a second
When the smudge stick
Shows symbols of horns on fire
And then returns to a smudge stick again
To remove all negative energy
Then you will know the time has come
Saddle the horses while the tanks are coming
Be the warrior for the chariots of fire
For Roman times are coming
Whose cloaks stream out behind as they forge
Their way into battle
Who is leading the army on horseback
Brandishing a flag I do not recognize
Except that it is red for the flag is angry
Not hiding emotionally red flag to a bull
It seems to have a sickle symbol on it

24. 09. 2021

The spell is broken trust in spirit to guide you
Out of what remains on the ground
Which is the carnage from the spoils of war
There is a blue butterfly it is like looking at the sky
Through a window shaped like a butterfly
The colors are very bright and very real
You can feel them through the lenses
Stay grounded little ones
Grounded grounded grounded
But not locked down
The ground beneath your feet
Can rise up to meet you
Half way when you walk upon it
There will be a gift by next Easter

26. 09. 2021

Light up the candelabra to unconditional love
Congratulate and celebrate
Those who are able to achieve it
The mindset has been broken
The pavements on the streets
At night are black and empty
Because people have
Retreated into their minds
Behind closed doors
When are the ten days of darkness
Where the light that shines
Comes from within
Slowly the trailblazers
And soothsayers will find another way
To celebrate the new day
Satellite dishes pizza cafes and plates
What is the purpose of all this
If it comes too late
Within the candle burns
The soul is not extinguished
Inside the human being
But more visible than ever
On a dark night

27. 09. 2021

A hand in a plastic glove is brandishing a branch like a wand
That is still alive like the wands card in the tarot deck
The branch has a medieval quality with leaves growing from its side
Meaning new growth from older times
Remembering where we come from
Meanwhile the hand is separated from the living branch
By a plastic sheath sanitizing glove such is the madness
Of the crazy war we are in that makes us afraid to be living and alive
Take off the glove and feel the wood to re merge with nature
And allow the sap from the branch to leak into your skin
So you can become one and stop brandishing the branch like it is a weapon
Going forward the climate change agenda will eventually come full circle
Because we can only insulate ourselves from being part of nature for so long
So gloves off and merge like you once did back in history
So that nature can absorb you back into its arms
And nurture you until you remember you are one
And on feeling it you re empower yourself

05. 10.2021

All manner of things are on the move now
Sputnik from out of space now landing
UFO and UAP now circling as well
There is a sense of the solar system in action
This is no ordinary war
The light bulb above your head emits a strange radiation
There are signals from out of space
Out of normal electrical devices
Out of range or out on the range
The battle cry is not heard outwardly but internally
The animals in the fields are hearing it
Go out on a dark night
And share the night sky with them for they will tell you
Many more secrets revealed in plain sight
Are not found on your internet but under the night sky
Shalom beloved Archangel Michael
And the light embodiment spectrum of the seven of heaven

06. 10. 2021

A raven or large black bird flying over the image
Of a DNA strand wrapped around a sword
Symbol of medicine a water container
With a vapor coming out what seems to be a
Window into a brighter backyard
The numbers 2 and 4
Are jumping up in sequence
A candle burning and a child's drawing
Stick figure of a person that tells a story as it is unraveling
About the mysteriousness of life
An old moped scooter
Hiding a black crystal at the foot tray
All manner of things are yet to be made known
Lying at our feet
An oriental round house and a garden retreat
A giant A turns into a tunnel with which to funnel out
What could be DNA strands
So many things are coming our way
On this roundabout half lit this circus of life
In which we are playing

19. 10. 2021

A four leaf clover and a bulldog clip
A star with a tail emerging
From and re entering a box
A brilliant spot of light
Tells me the fog is lifting
There is a wish beginning to form
Between humanity and the universe
A wish to climb out of the box
Of our pre conditioned world
To a point where we can be guided
To a new universal understanding
That links our planet
To our solar system and beyond
The tail of the star leaves a gas
But eventually as the fog is clearing
The night sky becomes visible
For the first time we are free
On the other side of the box
Humanity has finally
Freed itself from enslavement

20. 10. 2021

A willy wagtail made its nest
On my hills hoist clothes line
Willy wagtails on skis
Dealing with the artificial slopes in life
And making them work
A black bird with red eyes
Turns its eyes to me
And communicates as if to say
I acknowledge you are there
Even when I am about to go and have a busy day
Then he flies away
The birds will acknowledge us
As we can acknowledge them
Even on a busy day
When we are about to go to work
That way we can remember
We are one and we are integrated with nature
That is something they do not forget
And neither should we
It's all about the remembering
We are all together on this one big planet
Making it work and keeping balanced
In spite of change

24. 10. 2021

Looking through the workings of an attachment
Whose central part has been removed
Made of plastic designed to be a plastic flower
For plastic hope in a plastic world
But the centre has been removed
Now and the flower is gone
All that are left are fake flowers
And the obvious lack of usefulness of it all
Useless piece of landfill is all that's left of the fake world
That was planned for us
But we cannot see into its workings
While it is surrounded by fake leaves
That screen the fact that the core is missing
Unless we can turn the flower until we have an aerial view
From here we see the core is gone
The fake world needs to be flushed
From its centre with water
This will cleanse the artefact from its artificial purpose
So that it can be removed and transformed
Maybe then we can turn it back
Into a sprinkler to irrigate the earth
While we concern ourselves
With natural living once more

29. 10. 2021

The image of the vibration of Om
Has a gold and yellow centre in space
The importance of that vibration
That has lifted our energy for eons
The darkness of the end of Red October 2021
No one really knows what is happening
The war between the deep state
And humanity is not revealed to us except in our dreams
When we have anxiety like I did last night
After watching a video zoom on Dictator Dan
And his permanent State of Emergency
Pandemic plan to set a precedent in Australia
I remember as a child being obsessed with an image
Of a giant eating a tiny adult male now I know that symbol
As a premonition of these times
The need for conscious awakenings are obvious now
If I let the horrors overwhelm me I will be consumed
So I resist consciously but I am so tired today
Electrical storms followed by grey days are an energy zap
These are the last days of the ones we call the tyrants
For much changes in the passing of an emperor
Quote from earlier writings before I understood
We can only be consumed by a hologram
Of the original fear in this time now

Note to myself:
During my prayer ancient Egypt came into view and I thought about the Nephilim giants of my childhood image.
Once we roamed the earth visible to each other and now if time is a construct.

They still occupy parallel realities in quantum thought.
We are still walking with their shadow in third dimension.
So surely we have the power to shrink the shadow and cast
Off like we do our own shadow.
All must be taken into account at this point.
How we got here and how we got to here.
All disclosures will eventually fit together.
And not contradict each other. Then it will be time.
The true time not a time warp.
At the point where we will know the truth we will be
grounded but not locked down.
The deep state doesn't so much care about whether we know
but whether we can do anything about it.
We must fight for the disclosure with all we have
which is much more than we think we have except for time

02. 11. 2021

A babies dummy that could be a respirator for a tiny child
I see the child with bare legs in the baby stroller
There are crystalline forms that transform
Into a modern suburban house
Is this a sign of all we have lost or all we have to regain
In a world that has gone temporarily insane
An amethyst stone Is made into a ring
The stone is dark and the clasps are weak
People are trying to survive
This apocalypse in any way they can
Crystalline rocks and things made from it
Seem to be the key to self healing
Hay in a field stacked for a bonfire
As it is close to Halloween
Clearing the ground litter to regrow a crop
Life as we know it now is what it is and what it is not
There is an object like a healing utensil
That resembles a lotus with a light
At its centre that shoots out a frequency
A broken crystal bowl on a plinth
In a museum or gallery
Even the broken fragments are precious artefacts
Something about moon energy from wax to wane
Is connecting us back to the natural magnetic grid anyway

03. 11. 2021

A city skyline melts in the middle of the horizon
Like plastic and liquefies into the ground or water in front of it
And then turns into an image or a mold of an artifice from byzantine times
A monk or holy person with a halo two monks surrounded by halos
Begin to move towards each other in combat and then become one
Like ideologies that melt into one from dual or false narratives
Perpetrated over eons
A stained glass window divided into four parts
Each makes reference to current canceling of cultures
As there is nothing in each part
A hand reaches up as if to put something there but
The jaws of a strange carnivorous fish eating smaller fish
That have laid in its jaws has multiple teeth
The world as we know it is unraveling
There are those who would seek
To rewrite their own narratives Into antiquity
A bird comes with a quill in its beak
To write on paper something that
Was not written from earlier times
Sometime during the eighteenth century
Fragments of stories and images in florescent silhouette
Float down in a cave a crack becomes visible
At the top of the entrance to the underground where light streams in
A cloud or a bomb shaped like a cloud hovers over a country town
And a plume changes into a giant fan
One half of an old fashioned stopwatch like what was used in
Lewis Carroll's Alice in Wonderland is symbolic
Saying half the stories from the rabbit hole

Have been revealed or just a little more
The stop on the watch could be pushed until no more is revealed
But the watch is a black silhouette against a blue sky this time
Like a giant in the clouds we are just over half way
To exposing the lies and manipulations over centuries of human existence

09. 11. 2021

A dark ornate mirror and a reflection of a lazar thin line
That cuts through the darkness like a blinding continuous flash
All manner of darkness within the human soul has been cut through
As I look at the lazar it widens into an opening until there is no dark mirror
And only the opening to another world beyond mirrors reversing the black hole
It still has the power to pull all that I am into it a world of matter from a mirror of antimatter
So many things that were hidden in the darkness are now visible
We have nowhere to hide from our own darkness and nowhere to hide from the darkness of others
Trust in the process and recognize the cleansing true love and balance of and within self
Are paramount now so enjoy the ride

Meditation the same night with class on zoom
A poem came through
There is a white rose of love and peace
Like the dove of peace compassion
The dove of peace is the love of peace
Calibration tool is measuring our alignment
And readjusting our angles to fit our divine purpose on earth

11. 11. 2021

A loose bolt without the screw turns into a spinning top
In the atmosphere of space if you look down its centre
It's a mechanical time tunnel bolted to a child's tricycle wheel
An old fashioned magnet is pointing towards me
It is trying to attract me
Much like the bolt needs the screw to become part of the bigger whole
But for a moment I thought I was the bolt being magnetized
Laws of attraction and laws of the universe laws of nature
Where human nature is bound by these things that can fit together
To make a larger whole

15. 11. 2021

A fat Buddha is on a billy cart
While mickey mouse is now flying the sleigh at Xmas
All our religious icons and festivities
Mixed up with other narratives or are they
As the false narratives are exposed
Some have held onto for millennia
There is a sense of pop and satire
In our festivities and celebrations
Santa just kicked arse with his boot
But he is walking from behind
The Xmas tree in plain sight
The man behind the red coat and white beard
Is exposed and asking us to get over it
We are so addicted to our mythologies
That when one dies we create another in our heads
We are emotionally invested
In perpetuity within our rituals
Time to break the mass that turned black
Time to stop seducing our children and feeding them
Into the mouths of giants who eat them for breakfast
Time to see the satanic rituals mixed into popular culture
For what they are and break free from the hypnosis

16. 11. 2021

The mortgage lenders are profiting from our losses
A house is not a house any more
The fallen swords on the ground in the tarot deck
Someone is making away with what they are stealing
There is a brand name
But I am not familiar with its corporation
How naïve we have been how incredibly trusting
And naïve we have been time to wake up stand up
And grow up and take back our sovereignty

17. 11. 2021

Some variety of daisy we used to pull the petals off once
She loves me she loves me not
A babies rattle and thoughts of how we are so addicted to being
Answerable to those who feed us and forget that we are
Able to speak directly to the divine answerable to no one but ourselves
Human nature or what we have called human nature is about to change
Intercepted by an Artificial Intelligence inserted into our brains
Created by those who have and those who have no mental stability
The only thing that can save us now is our maturity
Brought about by adversity for some
Not adherence to some guru or master of the past
But by reigniting our own divine spark
No matter what the situation we find ourselves in
At this point in time

18. 11. 2021

Great Omniscient Divinity reignite the flame of my own divinity
That I may see myself as a flame within an all knowing flame
Of life existence and understanding
Remind me of who and what I truly am so that I may stay forever in love
With the wonder and mystery of all that is and not become preoccupied with my own
Life and death experience to such an extent that I shut everything else out
Fear is whittling away at us all in this time of transition
To the magnificent expansion of our planet
Like we are stuck in the birth canal
All humanity is feeling and speaking about it in one form or another
Some are struggling with it more than others
And taking the ultimate painkiller to end their own rebirth
Self abortion and shortening of their own life experience on earth

19. 11. 2021

All kinds of triangles within triangles
Divine geometry and sacred geometry
Cross section of an obtuse angle upside down like a number 7
That turns into a Z across the infinite triangles behind
And then a re calibration tool
At some point I see the A for Artificial Intelligence
With a biological umbilical chord emerging from it as though
It is being pulled through an arch
It is the lunar eclipse in Scorpio November 18 2021
I'm not sure what these images mean
But they are in divine geometric language
I need to record them while the human biology
And human genome are at stake
There is work going on behind all that the deep state could alter
We need to remove the malign
And restore to remove and realign us back
To the perfect geometry of the universe

24. 11. 2021

Feeling electric energy depletion
While these storms are in the atmosphere
Between lunar and solar eclipses in Sagittarius
A paperclip connects to a fake flower
The flower is a bit like a gerbera
I was feeling something
Had to be removed from me or my clothing
That comes from a fake outside world
The Nephilim are giants from ancient Egyptian days
When we co existed in plain sight together
Once we unpin the symbols of a fake narrative
And look behind to find what is natural
That's where we may also find the supernatural
And realize what has diminished us and depleted our energy
Drained by lies

25. 11. 2021

My mother is here for my birthday
Visit from the other side
She is standing back as she usually does
There is a wheel tyre that turns into a cats face
I think it is a lioness symbolic of my strength
For my strength in adversity
There is a package on a launching pad
Like a rocket but it is a giant microphone
As the wrapping comes off
It turns into some kind of Ankh
Mounted on a stand but the centre has lit up
Energy transference from ancient times
There is a cats paw that reminds me of Thomas
Who is also on the other side
It is a special reminder of love and strength

27. 11. 2021

A wrist band that is a time travel device
That turns into a clock
That can take us back and forth
Or shoot us at a right angle
Into another dimension
Who needs a space ship
When we have this
We are our own spaceship
No matter what form we become
Going forward or backwards
As we see it in linear timing
But in reality it is a dimension switch
Which is why the right angle
That shoots us out of our cosmic angle
Orbiting our gravity in another time zone
Or orbiting the gravity of another being
Of like minded attraction
Drawn together by our consciousness
Preoccupation and unconscious desires
In the time and space
We occupy as we know them

02. 12. 2021

The peasants are storming the porte cull-is of the castle
They are at the draw bridge they are storming the gates
With a battering ram and all kinds of activity making ammunition
A different kind of mask this time it's face shield armor
A person is having a face mold made to fit the shield
Leaving only the mouth and throat free
There is so much upheaval in the atmosphere in Australia
Today is the day they decide if the bill in Victoria will give
Dictator Dan the power and if the rest of the states will follow
Today the people all over Australia have had enough
Finally they are over the apathy
This is the mirror image of storming the bastille in France
We have to get the bastards out of office
And like the French Revolution we have to
Take down our government
So our governments cannot take down us

07. 12. 2021

The lunar to solar eclipse of December 2021
Has been a time of realignment and re calibration
To the source of all being
Only when those two things have occurred within ourselves
Can we feel our energy come back and we can spin into the vortex
Of ever expanding space in the universe
There is an old sailing ship with its flags and sails up
But it seems to be jet propelled
Moving much faster and directly with a sense of purpose
Cutting through the obstacles with ease
As if there are no obstacles for indeed with this force
Of balance and realignment and sense of direction
Nothing can stop its movement on the ocean of possibilities
Clean direct jet propelled white sail and a red emblem
A force to be attuned to not reckoned with

10. 12. 2021

A corner of the pineal gland has cleared and lit up
A cleansing that is visible to the inner eye
With this insight I can watch and work with clearing the rest
Until the pineal gland becomes completely visible to my inner eye
Another dimension of knowing is being returned to me
I am now scanning my inner organs to return to full health
I will document this process for this process will be
One that many others can follow as many have done before me
To return to a state of divine consciousness
Through such a simple de-calcification
I have glimpses of an inner landscape becoming three dimensional
Where my senses are active like wearing virtual reality glasses
Without needing the apparatus
No wonder the dream time becomes awake time
And awake becomes the dream
How amazing to be able to move in both dimensions
To trip the light fantastic consciously at once eyes open eyes shut
I see hands joining in prayer pose and a hand putting on a P.P.E. glove
Two opposite things a hand can do when hands are busy
And aware of the mind behind the action
We should be sure footed in order for our feet to be swift

14. 12. 2021

I am seeing a future city cleaning up the waves from
Artificial satellites around skyscrapers
There is a fountain with water around the rim of a bowl
Spring wound as a geometric pattern with a rod in the centre
It radiates a frequency conducted by the geometric pattern of the water
That will clear and disperse the microwaves that are frying our biology
And emitting radiation around our cities and buildings
This invention can be attached to the top of buildings
As well as in the parks on the ground
It is to ionize and neutralize the harmful rays
It seems to run on free energy using some sophisticated solar base
Where water absorbs and transforms the negative energy
With some sort of Tesla coil at the centre
It will be necessary to use all the reverse engineered technology for good
On our civilizations return to restored balance
And to remove the harmful rays instantly
Once the technology has been rescued
From the hands of evil doers

11. 01. 2022

A Christmas tree looks like a ghost against a dark sky
The ghosting of Christmas
This year wasn't the celebration we thought it would be
Followed by a new years eve where Big Ben in UK forgot to chime
The whole planet is moving into a new paradigm
Santa sleighs and reindeer look more like sideshows at a circus
There is a growth of pine trees in a circle in real time the pine trees
Were chopped behind my block exposing me to a caravan park
Symbolic of what is exposed when the ceremony is removed
While some people cling tightly to their fantasies and beliefs in a bubble
Out there somewhere a new truth is emerging that we will only see
When we have thrown away our toys

14. 01. 2022

Things are ditsy again
Last week I couldn't think
A lot of us were like that
Making bad decisions
But today is clearer
The writings wouldn't come easily
But they are reconstructing now
I'm seeing bits a pieces of the bigger picture
A wheel off a bed roller
A chime with its chimer laying crosswise
A strange light but only part of it I think it's circular
Think we have been shrouded
In the atmosphere
Too many people so tired and only want to sleep
Grey skies and strange weather
Our consciousness is temporarily blocked
It's freeing up now
And bits are coming through
Like the intel on social media
It has been so mixed
With fake news so infiltrated
But it's clearing up now
Like the weather

15. 01. 2022

The Vatican is close to the surface of exposure
For all its crimes perpetrated in the black goo
The crown is only visible as an artifact
But not on any ones head
The fall of the great controllers the empires and the evil ones
Have begun to be fulfilled
There was no strike of Big Ben at midnight 31st Dec 2021
There at the will of the people and the bell not tolled
At the strike of the clock for whom it never tolled at midnight
Symbolic of the absence of the heads of our empires
Who controlled us from behind
For they are all gone now and it is only the shadow
Of the monarchical empire that plays out in 2022
For the paradigm has shifted out of the hands
That once controlled its contents and its populations
The true rats are now caged and about to be exported
From the old earth as we knew it
That was the end of the world as we knew it
And this is the birth of the new millennium
As we will come to understand it humanity has won
The eye of Osiris appears between the cracks
In a wall that could have been a pyramid
But it has fallen to the bottom
Reminding us what was done has now become undone

20. 01. 2022

There are a pair of lungs grey as the sky above
Internal organs and a spinal column
Stretching up into the sky
Until the lungs become clouds
Searching for fresh air and light
There is a foghorn blaring
From the left of the picture I see
Like a megaphone of ever expanding vibration
But I hear no sound deafening silence
There is a metallic being rising from beneath me
It is an AI creature from a scifi film
Rising to compete artificially with the natural world
The trees are blowing in a gale force wind
In the artificially created weather zone
In the middle of a Dr Seuss style truffula tree
There is a smiling Cheshire cat face breaking through
It is not malign and promises to reverse climate change
A promise of sunshine behind the illusion created
And an end to the bleak simulation
Being perpetrated upon us

23. 01. 2022

Tree stump chopped down with a modern day saw
Garlic in abundance to hang over my door
A sickle moon but it is mounted on a stand
I am blowing up balloons with my own breath
And my own hands
If there's a reason for us to celebrate
May it be because it's not too late
The waters in the pitcher now
The signs are on our gates
A crack beneath the dungeon door
The lights are streaming in
Our self imposed imprisonment
Has made us go within
To reignite the flame inside
And rise up from our chair
Fling open doors and go outside
To breathe in real fresh air

24. 01. 2022

An old fashioned artists impression
Of a devil like a huge tree
Spreading its limbs out
Like a giant against a grey sky
Changes into a dead rose petrified
Emerging out of the darkness of a cave
Followed by a gold nugget
Fashioned like a manifestation
It is a sign to be careful what we wish for
Be careful what we focus on
It is also a symbol of the passing
Of all these negative images
And the promise of a new world
Like a gold nugget emerging
Out of the fear of the darkness
To celebrate a new dawn of consciousness
We have turned the corner
And turned on the light
It seems as we realize how we manifested
Our own worst dreams and nightmares
In the first place

31. 01. 2022

An ear on its own listening the breath of life breathing
I see a surfboard preparing for the wave
To ride the crest is to be in the now
The way to fulfill our true destiny
Not hampered by past illusions for the past is gone
It is time now to move on
The bells of destiny are calling
Ride the crest of the wave
Ride it ride it for there is your energy and purpose
Your true divine purpose for living
Unshackled from the chains of the past
The chains have broken away unhandcuffed
The true birth of the new millennium has begun
Rise up little one Rise up Rise up
To meet the crest of the wave

12. 02. 2022

My heart is beating to the sound of an African drum
There is a poppy growing
In a field on its own
Symbol of the first fallen
From the experiment
The sun is on the single flower
And the energy is high
Like the sun in the sky
A fan blows sideways
And birds screech in real time
Reaching into my altered state
Like an alternative reality
Humanity has woken up
No longer guided
By spreadsheets and flowcharts
On a virtual reality tablet
There is a sense of optimism
In spite of the doom and gloom theories
In mainstream media
We are only waiting
For the media to catch up now
It will keep sounding the war cry
Although the battle is nigh over
It is time little ones it is time the battle is WON

01. 03. 2022

I am at Heather's face there under the ground
A fly has landed on her black eye
I am asking myself and Michael why oh why
Was she buried alive
When the mountainside gave way
In Upper Wilson's Creek
At 4 am on 28th Feb 2022
He is asking me to hold my hands together in prayer
And I do as it calms me down
I see two other hands held in prayer next to mine
As my hands open out they reveal a brilliant radiance
It is a jewel revolving and expanding
There will be more of us to raise the energy
And as time as we know it proceeds more again
As this is the force of love
Between two sides of our brain
This is the true ascension as we know it
Once we return to Father Mother God where all of us unite
Like a brilliant radiant revolving jewel
Manifested between our prayers
And our love and our united focus

02. 03. 2022

I see Michael's urn at the gully end of Heather's block
As I am saying my prayers for Heather's eventual rescue
I am seeing a blue tarp but I think it is a stretcher
They are walking up to where her house once was
From the gully it seems
All Michael's legions are walking with them
For this massive air rescue cleanup of the rubble
I am praying they will not get to her too late
Is there hope in all our hearts for now
We live in the now and we can only do
What we can only do

08. 03. 2022

A clump of cherries turns
Into a bunch of grapes
Being handed out from the back
Of an old fashioned truck
I am transported to the floods
Where the arm of God
Extends through the army of the people
On the street with nothing to do
But to help their fellow human beings
Compassion in the hearts now
That the trauma is receding
With the mud and debris of the floods
That have been washed from shore to shore
To inland sea like a wave
All power to the people
To set each other free
From yet another onslaught
And another kind of tyranny

10. 03. 2022

Hands held together like clenched fists
In prayer holding on then turn into a posy
Of flowers at a funeral
With a cross that emerges from two fingers
Held up saying f..k you
And two weeks or two months
There is another red flag
And the people are again
Storming at the castle gate
Two white knitted neck scarves
Laid across each other on a red background
After the artificially generated storms
I see a sea of people the people are uprising
Angry and now with nothing to lose
And now they are more organized
Some one is fishing in the filthy storm water alone on the bank
A spinning top is moving very fast but still visible
It may be gaining momentum
In a storm water drain of the human sewers in Sydney
The D.U.M.B.S. will be brought to light
Very soon what stinks of dark malevolence
Will be laid out on the grass above the ground
In the sunlight of days to come
I am tired so tired it has been such an exhausting process for all of us

15. 03. 2022

The lights are out in the Northern Rivers
There is nobody home
Abandoned buildings and lifestyles
Businesses destroyed forever
No sign of life and no rescue squads
They have all left
A week ago today
Life as we know it in the disaster zones
Floated away in a torrent
In a river of sewerage
Dead cattle and marooned people
Bodies in the water
The stench of death is overwhelming
Two weeks ago
Life as we knew it back then
Teaming with life
The hustle and bustle of people
And events too busy to notice
The ominous clouds on the horizon
Perpetrated by an even darker force

20. 03. 2022

There is a baby chick sitting
On a twig outside the nursery nest
It is ready to fly and yet it is not moving
But sitting looking out from the comfort
Of its familiar surroundings
It is contemplating the inevitable
Flying to new horizons
But for now it is sitting looking out
This is a super important point of contemplation
For not all change has to be forced
Upon us by devastation and chaos
It is far better to gather strength for flight
That is self actualized
And motivated from within
Be still in your current environment
For the change is inevitable for us all
Where nothing can stay the same forever
We must all eventually
Take flight into new horizons

18. 06. 2022

In the New Normal
My bum is my new lung
And my lung is my new bum
I wear a mask when I walk past
No oxygen creeps underneath
Cause I'm breathing from my arse
I buy 10,000 toilet rolls to sanitize my hands
In case a teeny bit of arse hole
Infects my respiratory gland

This poem was not written under meditation but encapsulated the toilet roll panic at the beginning of the pandemic. After this time things continued in intensity as the masking and lock downs started to roll out. It seemed the rest of humanity was in shock and could only think base survival. Something in me discovered humour and compassion which is also why the writings under meditation began in earnest

Acknowledgements

The Reverend Michelle Baum Founder of Spritualist Church North Shore Sydney Australia
Thankyou for encouraginging me to write down my personal meditations during lockdown 2020-2022. Without your spirit guides prompting me to start writing again these writings would not have happened.

The late Heather and Michael Scott for Michaels "Writings for Humanity"
I am forever grateful for your divine inspiration and insight into humanity. I am truly honoured to have enjoyed our friendship over the thirty years I knew you both. You will remain with me in my heart and soul as my peers soul family and my mentors throughout the rest of my journey on this earth.

Front cover by Gail Fay, Artistic Director of Springboard Productions P/L, Melbourne. Winner of the 2000 Australian Achiever Award (for excellence in Advertising, Marketing & Public Relations).
Thankyou for being my new friend and neighbour who bought the converted church I love to visit. I am grateful to you for taking the time to be part of the magic of the journey that has helped these projects come to fruition over the last two years. I have truly appreciated your imput into my projects.

www.ingramcontent.com/pod-product-compliance
Lightning Source LLC
Chambersburg PA
CBHW071943090426
42740CB00011B/1806
* 9 7 8 0 6 4 8 2 3 6 9 2 4 *